Creative Writing

Creative Writing

E. Blackburn

authorHOUSE®

AuthorHouse™
1663 Liberty Drive
Bloomington, IN 47403
www.authorhouse.com
Phone: 1-800-839-8640

Published by AuthorHouse   08/24/2012

ISBN: 978-1-4772-1538-8 (sc)
ISBN: 978-1-4772-1539-5 (e)

The cover picture refers to Belshazzar's feast cited in the Bible, Daniel 6 verse 25. Is that not, "Creative Writing" par excellence?

CONTENTS

FOREWORD

The stories and poems written here are the product of many tasks which were given to me, or suggested, however vaguely, by a teacher of Creative Writing.

There would have been more but the Wirral Borough Council, decided not to further subsidise the classes.

The students were mostly "Young" Senior Citizens paying £75per head, for a ten week course, three hours per week.

Thanks go to teacher Ms Lisa Blower. Google her.

ANYTHING

Twenty-three years ago I retired, after working forty years for the same company. Not being a retiring type, I felt that I had to keep the grey matter in working order on the principle that you use it or lose it. There was a course in DIY. which I did. There was 'Computers for Beginners', which I did. Then followed, 'Computers for Experts'. What next? 'Creative Writing'. Try that? The Booker Prize beckons. Move over Jeffery, I have a book signing.

At the age of seventy-three I signed on at the local school to learn 'Creative Writing Skills.' Some students were years younger than I and I feared that keeping up to them, each with a fist full of A-levels, was not going to be easy. I had heard somewhere that everyone has at least one book in them, and on entering the class I felt as though mine was right there, undigested, below my ribs. I tried to comfort myself with the knowledge that I had been to places and seen things that they would never see. In my time I had featured as the main character in two books. They were my headmaster's and sergeant major's black books. I was as well equipped as Kipling. I have been 'On the Road to Mandalay,' and into the Moulmein Pagoda, and I know 'There's a Burma girl a-sittin,' but I am not sure she still thinks of me.

We had a taskmistress, who gave us copious tasks to do at home. She had us imagine ourselves in all sorts of situations with equally weird characters. I can now understand why some great arty types take to 'Wacky Bacy' aids, to enhance their creative skill. Our Mentor soon had the class move from one-hundred word efforts, to us each aspiring to write a magnum opus.

At one session our instructor asked us to write some dialogue. She then relented and said, "If you feel uneasy about writing dialogue, then you might like to write an autobiographical piece relating to 'my first date, pay day, driving lesson, kiss, etc." Her list was extensive, and, running out of ideas, she said, "Well really, you could write about My First Anything."

Well really, I could not think of how to start to write about *anything*. You see, I could not recall when I received my first *anything*, but I could recall the first time that I learned of its existence. I was about three years old and Father Christmas was inviting me to choose an item from his array of goodies. My mother had paid two shillings and six pence, which was the top price, and this allowed me to select a toy from his entire catalogue. I must have taken a long time to make up my mind.

I distinctly remember him saying, "You can choose *anything*."

My mother, growing impatient, said, "Oh, choose *anything*," but I didn't, I chose a fire engine. However, there must have been an *anything* for me to select.

Later, nearer to Christmas, the church wanted toys for poor children. My mother asked me what toy I would give. Not being able to decide, I asked her for advice and she said, "Oh, give them *anything*."

I can't remember looking among my toys for an *anything*, but I gave them my teddy. Again I must have possessed an *anything* without knowing it.

Once, nearing the end of the school day, my teacher enquired, "Have you learnt about *anything* today?"

He was not best pleased when I said, "No."

By about ten years of age I had become aware that *anything* is responsive to the five senses. I had assessed that it can be smelt, seen, heard, tasted and felt.

An *anything* must have a smell. I remember once arriving home with my Mum. On opening the door she enquired, "Can you smell *anything*?" I said that I could not but there was smoke coming from the hearth rug. Therefore, besides the smell of smoke she must have been able to smell this elusive *anything*.

Again an *anything* must also be visible to the naked eye. We were at the seaside looking into one of those telescopes and my Mum said, "Can you see *anything*?" I could not, and did not, and do not know what one looks like, but I could see a ship far out to sea.

A similar thing happened long ago with my Granddad. He had a cat's whisker radio, and on placing the earphone to my ear said, "Can you hear *anything*?"

Excitedly I said, "I can hear crackling and a man's voice."

"That's good," he said, but had I heard *anything*? At one time my Mum and I were sitting having our supper. We both took bites at our toast. She tightened her lips and pushed up her nose before saying, "Can you taste *anything*?"

Considering and chewing at the same time, I said, with my

mouth full, "I think the butter is going off, it must have been left in the sun all day." As there was nothing else for her to taste, I presumed that toast tastes like *anything*.

I was twelve years old when the dentist said to me, "Can you feel *anything*?" I merely grunted, but it gave me food for thought.

At the age of fourteen, my elder sister, on returning from a shopping trip, was asked by my Mum, "Did you buy *anything*?"

My sister said that she had not. How I wish that she had indeed bought an *anything*, as I would now know how to recognise one.

On reflection, it appeared that all my life everyone I had encountered knew or had had experience of an, *anything*. I seemed to be excluded.

My tutor had, because she said we could write about *anything*.

Only recently I became acquainted with a man whose wife said, "My husband can grow *anything*."

"*Anything*?" I enthused, "Where does he buy the seed?"

"He buys all his seed at Goredale Nurseries," she replied.

Off I went to Goredale Nurseries. I must have looked suspicious hanging around the huge array of seeds. Alphabetically, seeds of *anything* should have been near the top of their selection, but I could not see them.

An assistant offered to help. "What kind of seeds are you looking for?" she asked.

"Oh *anything*," I replied, cringing with embarrassment.

"Do you want vegetables or flowers?" Was she indicating that there were two types? This was news.

"At last!" I thought. If there were two types, I would try both, and blurted out, "Both!"

"Have you a large piece of land?" she enquired.

"About ten yards by twenty-five," I considered as I replied.

"In that case," she said, "that is about the size of an average allotment." She screwed her face up in thought saying, "You should be able to grow *anything* on a piece of land that size."

I thought, at last someone giving a positive statement about acquiring *anything*. I hedged, and chose to say. "Will you pick about six packets of *anything* for me please?" I said this because I still could not see a packet labelled *anything*.

She selected peas, beans, carrots, pansies, asters and salvia, adding, "You must read the instructions, because you may need to have a bit of heat to germinate them, but if you have a greenhouse, you can grow *anything*, anytime."

I thanked her, but did not mention that I did not have a greenhouse. The fact that I could not see *anything* on packets, other than 'peas,' 'beans,' etc. perplexed me. Believing her to know what she was talking about, I did not show my ignorance, so I took them home and planted them. I was rewarded with some lovely beans, carrots, and much praise for my asters, but furtively looking for *anything* did not bear fruit.

To my chagrin, my grandson, then twelve years, caught me looking among the plants and asked, "What are you looking for Granddad?"

"*Anything*," I said guiltily.

"Well," He said. I winced at his sassy riposte. "Have you found *anything* worth finding yet?" This, I thought, is more news. There are differing values to this *anything*. I wondered whether it was because it wears out, or is it size and quality?

Guiltily and sheepishly, I confessed my ignorance and told him of my quest. He must be far more enlightened than I, because he said, with much confidence and disdain, "Don't you know, 'ANYTHING'?"

On reflection, he had a point, I know nothing about *anything*, and therefore could not write about *anything*. But I gave my tutor this script. Ever helpful my tutor produced a magazine in which there was a competition. She said that they would probably accept one of my stories for the prize in their 'Short Story' competition. She followed with, "You won't win *anything* if you don't try."

"Wow!" I thought, after all this time, a chance to win and get my hands on an a*nything*. I could not let that pass.

But I didn't win anything.

*   *   *

It was a warm moonless night; whispers of cloud hid the stars, as four boys of the Eagle Patrol were making their slow progress in the darkness of the Welsh countryside. The group were on a seven-mile night-hike, each trying to gain yet another proficiency badge to be displayed on an arm which was already enveloped in trophies. They were allowed one storm lamp, a map and victuals as they thought fit. In this blackest of nights the only glimmer, and it was a glimmer, of light in the whole valley was that of their paraffin lamp. As they plodded on, taking care not to fall into ditches or miss any turnings, out of the blackness came a tall man, who was hardly visible in the small light but for the white of his seemingly large eyes.

One boy asked, "Are we on the road to Madog?"

"Yes," said the man, "about five-hundred yards on. I have just come from there."

From the darkness followed a, "Thank-you," and all went on their way.

A few steps further on, a whispering voice said, "That's funny, he said he came from Madog, but Skip said it's a deserted quarries village, and has been for seventy years."

Another voice in the darkness questioned, "And where could he be going? We have not passed any houses for at least two miles."

The lamp carrier skilfully avoided the questions and observed, "We must be at Madog now. Here's a wall. Well it was a wall, not much of it left."

Then, another whispering voice, "Let's see here, yes, it's a dilapidated house. Skip must have been right."

"I it about time we had a swig of that Coke," Jim suggested.

The four stopped to drink, none of them wishing to stray far from the light. The empty houses gave way to a shoulder high wall and from the darkness came, "I wonder what's over this wall? It's quite high and it isn't falling down."

"Don't bother looking over; it looks as though there has been a gate here."

Approaching the opening they could discern a wide, overgrown path. None cared to venture along it.

An excited voice said, "What was that?"

"A sheep sliding on the slate shards," said a confident voice.

A cautious voice offered an opinion, "It was straight ahead of us, there are no slate shards on the path."

Then a voice that dropped to a very quiet whisper, "Look over there, there are lights moving about."

There was quiet while they considered this statement.

In the darkness it was hard to judge distance, but not far away there were indeed some flickering lights.

Harry voiced the thoughts of all, "Come on, let's get a move on."

"There it is again!" a voice said excitedly.

But as they turned to go, the noise became clearly footsteps of someone or something coming towards them on the path.

A man and a woman appeared out of the darkness. The woman wore a black shawl and the man wore a white shirt. He had large whites to his eyes which their lamp picked out clearly.

Jimmy bravely plucked up courage to say, with a gulp, "How far is it to Madog?"

Without stopping or otherwise commenting the woman said, "You have just passed it, we live there."

"Thank you," said two voices in harmony.

But Harry asked a question which compounded all their thoughts. "Did you see the hat she was wearing?" he asked, "I'm sure it was a witch's hat."

David agreed saying, "I thought it was tall but didn't want to say it. Do you think she was a witch?"

Jimmy again tried to steady their nerves, "If it was a witch, she would have one of those familiars, you know a black cat or a rook." And as he said it, a small black dog ran out of the gate and turned to catch up with the pair.

The boys quickly made the three yards from the gate and the couple into twenty-three, but in the darkness it was difficult to keep to the road while in a hurry.

The wall came to an end with a stile, before continuing at a right angle away into the darkness. There was a footpath sign. David reached the lamp up to read, 'Mynwent.'

"Mynwent, where's that?" said Jimmy. "Is it on the map?"

They opened the map on the footboard of the stile and Harry found Madog. "We are here and going this way, and look there. That must be this footpath and the wall and that path where the man and woman were and" . . . His voice dropped, stopped and then whispered, "Look what is inside the wall, a cemetery with the word 'Mynwent' in italics. Mynwent must mean cemetery."

All conversation dropped to a whisper.

David ventured to say, "But that man and woman came out of the cemetery and those lights are over there are in the cemetery. What would anybody be doing in a cemetery at this time of night, if they were not ghosts or maybe Vampires?"

"Or Zombie with those eyes," whispered Michael.

All four put on extra speed but stopped when Harry pointed to more lights moving on the hills at the other side of the valley, saying, "There are dozens of them."

"What could they be?" asked Michael as he moved to Sardine status with Jimmy and Harold.

Jimmy, sensing Michael's fear said, "It doesn't matter what they are, let's get out of here as quick as we can." Fifty yards on there was another noise, coming nearer, and it was footsteps of more people ahead of them.

"Stop! Listen," whispered David.

All stopped and huddled around the lamp, really afraid to move; the steps came nearer. Then the footsteps stopped. There was silence. More lights moved across the fields to their left.

"What date is it?" asked Jimmy.

"May the first," said Michael, "why?"

It's not Halloween," said Jimmy, "anyway that's all rubbish about ghosts and it is only Saints that go walkies on 'All Saints Night'."

"Well if it's rubbish," said Michael, "why are we whispering?"

Jimmy did not answer this question but replied, still whispering, "Don't tell me that was St Winifred, out with a fancy man with a witch's hat and shawl. It was a tall hat on her head not a wimple."

"Who was St Winifred?" asked David.

"She is a Welsh Saint," replied Jimmy, "she has a shrine and is supposed to be buried over in Holywell, which is miles away from here. It is unlikely that she is walking about around here. All the pictures I've seen of Saints, they all have bare feet. So she would have sore feet if she had walked this far." Jimmy, ever the clever one continued in a confident tone but nevertheless still tending towards a whisper, "I was thinking that it is not Halloween, but there is also another night. It's called Walpurgis Night. On that night, the first of May, this night, they say that people get out of their graves. They go to their homes to visit their kinfolk. Some visit the Devil."

Taking the lamp from Michael he said bravely, but still in a low whisper, "Let's go and meet them." They moved off, Jimmy first and the others almost hanging on to him, not so much walking in his footsteps but almost in his boots.

They made about thirty yards, gaining courage with each stride, when the four said almost simultaneously and not in a whisper, "What the hell is that?" as voices from the fields on their left pierced the night.

In growing apprehension, they all huddled together. Their faces were now white in the lamplight, as they listened to the voices in an argument. It surely was an argument. Even though it was in Welsh, they were sure it was an argument.

Reluctantly they pressed on, hoping to pass the voices, which seemed to be moving further away into the fields to the left.

They stopped dead for a moment, then began to run when one of the voices clearly called, "David."

All the other words were in Welsh but the word David was repeated three times.

David was now in front, moving as fast as he could on the pot-holed, unmade road and in the darkness. Gasping they slowed down as they came to a metalled road and an argon street lamp, which gave very little light and still less comfort, as it was embraced in the leafy arms of a tree. Barely visible there was a rusting finger sign, 'Llareggub 3'

"Hey! We have only three miles to go," said Jimmy, as he put his arm around David who was still convinced that the voices had been calling to him in particular.

"Yes," said Harry, "but they are Welsh miles! It will be more like 5 English miles."

Spirits were rising, only to be dashed as they heard footsteps and voices as if an army were approaching. There were red lights and barking dogs all coming their way.

The boys froze, all choosing to stay under the street lamp.

Jimmy's words fell to whispering again, "The red lights could be cigarettes."

"Ghosts don't smoke, do they?" Harry questioned. This seemed funny and reduced some of the fear.

Jimmy now with the lamp-light hoping to reassure them said, "Oh! Yer, what about Holy Smoke?"

By this time, some men who had dogs were right upon them and one speaking in a low English voice said, "You are out late lads, it's getting near the witching hour, the show is nearly over, if you want a short cut to town come with us."

With that the boys took flight and ran off down the road at Olympic speeds, finally stopping out of breath, under another street lamp. This lamp gave off a more comforting light and thinking they were well away from the men with the dogs they somewhat relaxed. It was not long before their breathing steadied but their hearts kept thumping just as hard.

Jimmy's false courage clicked in as he asked as a way of encouragement, "Have we done that three or five miles yet? Let's have some more of that Coke."

They finished off the Coke and Harry took possession of the empty bottle saying, "It was a good thing that we chose Coke in this glass bottle instead of the Sprite in the plastic bottle. If a Ghost comes near me I'll smash its head in."

"Great," said Jimmy, "If we do see a ghost we can safely leave it to you."

Off they went again with spirits somewhat restored and confidence growing with each step until, approaching another solitary street lamp, they distinctly heard a voice calling, "Jim, Harry, Michael is that you?"

Again they froze. As fear engulfed them, they huddled together, even Jimmy's confidence was waning.

"Harry is that you?" came the voice again.

"That's Skip," said Michael as he started to run again, this time towards the voice and shouting, "Skip is that you?"

Skip made his way towards them saying, "You have made good time boys, you must have run all the way, and it was supposed to be a hike."

David, now consoled and walking close to Skip answered, "We did put a spurt on because we saw some ghosts."

"Well, we thought they were ghosts," corrected Jimmy.

Skip said with a wry smile, "So you saw some ghosts did you? Well I'll go along with that. It will make a fine camp fire yarn tomorrow night."

"No, we did see ghosts, they came out of a cemetery," insisted Michael.

Just then they passed under another lonely street lamp. Fastened to the post were some fly notices written in Welsh and English. David pointed to the notice and saying to Skip,

"Look, Madog village that must be the Madog you said was deserted."

"It is an uninhabited mining village," said Skip, as they all stopped to read the notice

Eisteddfod Pentref	Village Eisteddfod
a Dans Gwerin	and Folk Dances
Ferm Lloyd	Lloyd's Farm
Pentre Madog	Madog village
Dydd Sadwrn	Saturday
Saith o'gloch	7 o'clock

"The people were only coming and going all over the mountain to and from an Eisteddfod," added Jim.

"Even people coming out of a cemetery calling me?" said an unconvinced David.

"Every other person in Wales is called David or Huw. It was just someone was calling his friend," said Skip as he took the lamp from Michael. "What a yarn it will make at the camp fire!" he continued as he adjusted the wick of the lamp, "Make sure you add to it to make it a good long story. Now let's get a move on back to camp, there's ox-tail soup and toast waiting for you."

Jimmy asked, "Have we done enough to get our badge?"

"I should think so" said Skip, "but I think we will have to contact the Chief Scout to see if he can have a special 'Ghost Busters Badge' issued for you three. Now, let's get back to camp. There's Ox tail soup and toast waiting and then we'll get some shut eye."

* * *

When Humpty Dumpty enrolled in the Duke of York's Regiment, Dr Foster gave Humpty a medical examination. He found that Humpty had egg-stra sensory optical vision in that he was egg-sighted. This is very rare and usually it would occur in autistic persons, but they almost always possess a disability in some other function. Humpty's was more like Elf-sighted; the sight of those Elves who inhabit part of Middle Earth (in the Lord of the Rings.) Suffice it to say that he could see for egg-stra-ordinary distances.

Due to his egg-stra-ordinary sight he was henceforth used by the Duke as a spy, to scout out the land and report enemy movements.

Humpty had an uncle who was 'His Excellency the Governor of Lilliput', a province of the King of Hearts's realm.

Now, you know that in Lilliput there were, for years and years, constant wars between the Big Endions and the Little Endions. One side insisted that boiled eggs should be opened at the big end and the other side insisted on opening the egg at the more pointed end.

The King, tiring of this constant warring in his kingdom, discussed the matter with the Duke of York. The Duke suggested that they send Humpty to report and investigate why the two parties could not reconcile their differences. The Duke reminded the King that Humpty was indeed a nephew of the governor. He could pretend that he was holidaying with his Uncle, and with his Egg-stra-ordinary gifts of long-sight and insight he might see or hear something that could be the basis for reconciliation.

On the visit to his uncle in Lilliput, Humpty did apply his egg-stra-ordinary mind to the warring problem and wisely came up with a solution. In Lilliput they were paying too much attention to their taxes, or should I say egg-size. Humpty proposed that they should abandon all forms of egg-size, in other words abolish taxes.

In time all the nation would forget, and be glad to forget about egg-sizes. Thereafter peace would reign for ever after.

For this brilliant philosophical idea Humpty was acclaimed 'Peacemaker Egg-stra-ordinary,' and a day to be called 'Peace Day' was dedicated in his honour. This would be on his birthday. He was also to be given a Knighthood for his services to the Duke of York.

His investiture was to be on his birthday also.

Though there were no more wars impending, the Duke of York nevertheless kept his king's men in good practice.

One day Humpty was on the mirador at the top of the castle tower, signalling to the Duke as to which way he would need to go to find some sheep that a Miss Bo Peep had lost. Humpty had locked himself in the tower and brought the key up to the balcony. Right below him were the many, many bags of wool which the Black Sheep was assembling for distribution.

With his egg-stra-ordinary vision, Humpty could see the lost sheep far away. At such a distance it was difficult to signal instructions to the Duke. The Duke was unfortunately sending his men up and down the hills several times while the mutton-headed sheep ran hither and thither. Amid this turmoil, Humpty felt someone or something push him from the tower where he was standing.

Humpty fell onto the bags of wool belonging to the Black Sheep and was severely concussed. Of course everyone wanted to revive him. Many, nearly all, of the soldiers tried. The Duke also tried but Doctor Foster, who had fortunately just returned from a trip to Gloucester, succeeded by tapping Humpty on the cheek and saying, "Come on lad pull yourself together."

Everyone was asking who would have a reason to push such a nice person as Humpty off the wall?

Now there was a wise old Owl that lived in an oak, the more he saw, the less he spoke, the less he spoke, the more he heard, and Humpty wanted to be as clever as that wise old bird. This very erudite Owl had been Humpty's teacher. Humpty had never spoken to anyone about the many civic misdemeanours he had witnessed but, as he was sure that he had been pushed, he visited his friend, the wise old owl, to discuss who might be the malfeasant.

In discussing who might be guilty, Humpty told the Owl that by virtue of his amazing sight, he had witnessed the Sparrow when he shot the Cock Robin with the bow and arrow. He had also seen Incy Wincy Spider harassing young ladies, in particular one Miss Muffet. He told the owl how he had seen Tom, the Piper's son, run off with a pig. Another terrible fellow was Georgy Porgy, he was seen stealing kisses from right under little girls' noses. Humpty was also aware that the cat was on the fiddle.

He had also heard rumours that the Queen expressed concern

when she discovered that his Investiture Day and the Peace Day were differing dates, yet both were his birthday. She had gone berserk when told that Humpty had many birthdays whereas she only had two. She was reputed to have said, "Off with his head!" The Abbot of St. Martins was miffed with Humpty because he alleged that Humpty owed him five farthings. The Abbott had, in a fit of pique, instructed the bells of St. Martins to proclaim this debt every time they rang out at evensong. And he had threatened Humpty with violence, in that he would get a chopper to chop off his head. Only that morning Humpty had seen the Knave of Hearts stealing some of the Queen's tarts.

The Owl agreed that there were a lot of potential guilty parties, but nothing incriminating any of them to the pushing of Humpty. The Owl kept insisting on the facts. How did Humpty know he had been pushed?

Humpty was sure he had felt hands on his back, but nobody could have pushed him. He had entered the bell tower and had locked the door from the inside. He then took the key up the tower with him. He had placed the key on the wall beside him, while he did the signalling.

"But somehow somebody did get in to push you," said the owl, "Let us go and see this bell tower and its key."

They went to the tower and the Owl sniffed and examined the key. He found the key very sticky with traces of a spider web on it. They both deduced that Incy Wincy had had one of his eight feet in the deed, but would not have had the strength to push Humpty.

On inspection of the tower, there were excessive traces of gossamer on a drain pipe and these were more than would be necessary for the making of a web.

The Owl deduced that it would be possible for Incy Wincy to wrap up the key as he would wrap up a fly and move the key to the drainpipe. He could drop it to the ground where he would need an accomplice.

"Now," said the Owl "they found blood on your back?"

"I was not injured," said Humpty,

"But they say there was blood on your back," said the Owl, "It must have been the pusher's blood. Where are the clothes that you wore that day?"

Luckily Humpty's clothes had not been washed because; the

laundry maid had been incapacitated by a blackbird attacking her nose. On inspection of his jacket they discovered that the red stuff was in fact strawberry jam.

There could be no other explanation. The Knave of Hearts had stolen the tarts and must have been aware that Humpty had seen him. Then, still with sticky strawberry jam fingers, he had perhaps blackmailed the spider to help him in his dastardly deed.

The hunt was now on for the Knave of Hearts, and there was a report of a Cock Horse being stolen. Humpty espied the Knave at Banbury Cross. The Duke's men did not catch him at Banbury Cross but Humpty saw the Knave again by the river Severn where he was about to steal a beautiful Pea Green Boat belonging to a Pussy Cat. This time the Knave was caught by the Duke's men.

The King, who never liked the Queen's cooking, and although she had many servants working in her kitchen, she was an avid watcher of television cooking programmes and wanted to make the cakes and pies herself. The King really did not like her pastries and was secretly pleased that the Knave had stolen the tarts. In fact the King was glad that he would not be asked to eat any of those tarts. Doing the King such a favour certainly did not deserve having one's head cut off, so the King chose a more lenient punishment. He decreed that the Knave should do some community service. He ordered that the Knave must work for one of his subjects who needed some respite care. There was an old lady who had so many children she was at her wits' end. He must do the housework for her for the next the six months.

The Queen wanted a much more severe punishment for the Knave than the King had decreed. She kept shouting, "Off with his head! Off with his head!"

It was explained to the Queen that Humpty did not have multiple birthdays but did have many 'unbirthdays.' It was just one of the weasel words which he had made up, and each word meant anything he wished it to mean. (This, you know, is a common trait amongst courtiers and politicians of every country.)

People say that Incy Wincy hides away in the dark corners and is rarely ever seen. There are reports that he still appears in bathrooms now and then to frighten and harass ladies.

It was the eve of Christmas. A large object, rather like a flying oil refinery, as big as a football pitch was in fixed orbit high above the earth. It had large square sections connected by large pipes. These pipes seemed to be twisted in all ways like a snake's nest. This was no ordinary man-made construction, neither was it a natural object. It had been constructed by some other form of life that lived way, way beyond the edges of our galaxy; they were not native to our earth. It was, in fact, occupied by a crew of alien beings who were monitoring the strengths and weaknesses of us humans. Why they were doing this we did not know. We were not sure whether their intentions were for good or for evil. To do their investigation, they had seven blocks of highly technical machinery, the sort that we would call computerised. These beings were of the same height as humans, had a head, rather larger than a human's, with large eyes which stretched from the front of the face to where a human's ears would be; arms like a human with an extra elbow and legs similar. They were nearly like humans, or, humans are nearly like them. They were however an ergonomic improvement on the human structure. Their clothes were made of a silk material and were of the simplest design, being loose fitting and lacking style of any kind.

One of their machines, like a radar scanner, showed a 'something' on its screen. Excitement filled the station and in their method of communication, which was not any language spoken on earth, they queried what it might be. Focusing on the object, it appeared to be a human in a red and white garb, sitting on an earth travel machine with no feet or wheels. The motive force seemed to be from a team of unusual horses. The aliens had copies of all manner of earth information like encyclopaedias and other reference sources. No doubt they had access to Google and the World Wide Web. They quickly resolved the horses to be our reindeer, but could not find any reference to them substituting for horses and being able to defy gravity. The red-coated human confounded them. They watched this human and his travel machine, which seemed to be levitating. This indeed was some special human that they had not, as yet, encountered. They decided to bring him on board to make a closer investigation. This was done by training a green tracker beam, like a searchlight, on the object, then either by magnetism or suction bringing the thing into an air lock and then into the station. Once inside the craft the reindeer were going berserk, but one of the aliens did something akin to hypnotism and the reindeer were quiet. The red-suited man was not similarly subdued. He remonstrated, but at the same time he was frightened.

One of the aliens who looked exactly like a human spoke to him in English. "Don't be upset," he said, "We want to know more about you, you are a unique human. Who or what are you?"

"I am called Father Christmas, though it won't surprise me if you don't believe me. Many people are sceptical about my very existence and I have a very important job to do tonight and little time in which to do it."

The alien seemed to interpret this to his brothers and asked Red Coat, to explain this work that he was doing. Father Christmas explained how he goes about the world delivering toys and other nice things to children and sometimes adults.

The alien asked, "What do they pay for this service?"

"Nothing," said Father Christmas, "it is all for free."

After more interpretation and excited chatter among the aliens they accused Father Christmas of lying.

The alien said, "You must tell us the truth. Humans never do anything for free they are always greedy and selfish. That was the first thing we discovered about humans."

While this conversation took place other aliens were pulling parcels and bags from Father Christmas' wheel-less travel machine, examining it to see if they could find the levitation mechanism. Those emptying the sled, for that was what the machine really was, were amazed and confused. No matter how many bags and boxes they took from the sleigh it was always full. The great number of parcels and bags that had been removed were beginning to clutter up the station.

The alien told Father Christmas that they had a method of looking like humans while they went down to earth to investigate, but it wore off if they got cold and had to be brought back onto the parent ship, so they never went down to earth in winter. He said that it did not matter how many layers of clothes they wore they still got too cold. They had examined some black and white strange birds that seem to be able to survive in very, very cold parts of your Earth.

"They would be penguins," said Father Christmas. "Even humans cannot live in places that cold."

"We have made suits like the man who makes your motor tyres. We made them with lots of padding but it did not keep us warm and people down there paid too much attention to such an enormous man."

"Now, there you would be thinking about the Michelin man advertising motor tyres; he is not a real human," said Father Christmas.

Some others who looked human came to ask questions. One of them said, "We have looked for Father Christmas in the list of Catholic priests world-wide, and you are not mentioned."

Another said, "Father Christmas is not mentioned in De Brett's Who's Who."

"You are not in Webster's Dictionary," said another alien, "That is a book where all English words are listed."

"That is because you are looking in non-fiction books!" said an exasperated Father Christmas, "If you are looking in Webster's, look for 'Santa Claus'. Most people think I am imaginary fiction. Look in some children's books. Now, I must get on my way to the children before dawn."

There were now so many parcels scattered about the station that the aliens gave up and tried to put some back. They found that they could not put any back into the sleigh because it was always full to overflowing.

"You are not telling the truth," said a very important looking alien, "You are real; you have a method of travel that no other earthling has; you have a box that never empties; you say that you give millions of toys and sweets to children, free! You do not get cold; you are not mentioned anywhere in the great books of the earth and you tell us to read children's books."

Father Christmas thought hard and enquired, "If you cannot go down to earth in the winter when it is cold, you might not have heard of me."

"We have not mastered the way you humans can live in the cold," said the important alien who was obviously above a captain of the spaceship.

"I can help you with that problem if you let me get on with my work tonight and let me go to my sleigh." Father Christmas was allowed to go to his sleigh and he took out an airman's suit with electrically heated fur lining, he offered it to an alien to wear.

The alien put it on and Father Christmas switched on the heating, after a minute or two the alien said, "I am melting."

"If you ever go to earth in our winter you would not see one of these suits because they are secret and only for aircraft pilots," explained Father Christmas, who then begged to be let on his way.

The captain insisted that if the suit is so good then his aide, with the suit, must go with Father Christmas to try it out.

Father Christmas did not object, but explained that owing to the time he had now lost he would not get to all the children in time.

"What exactly do you have to do?" asked the captain.

Father Christmas told him in detail that he must visit all the children and if possible get down the chimney with the toys. Sometimes the front door was left open for him in houses where there was no chimney or where the chimney was blocked up. Father Christmas also said how worried he was that they had taken so many toys and parcels out of his sleigh. They could not get them back into the sleigh. Those toys had to be delivered, but how?

The captain calmed Father Christmas saying, "I, in turn, can help you with that. If your suit works and my aide stays warm we can deliver the toys that are here. We can ZAP the toys into the houses from here and we will work all night on it, but if your suit does not work they will be Zapped into outer space."

Father Christmas asked, "What is meant by 'Zapping'?"

"It is one of your earth words which we have adopted," said the captain, "In English words, we 'Metamorphose' the items. That is we change them into their atomic particles, then beaming them down what you earthling would call a laser beam. At their destination they are reconstructed into their original form. We call that Zapping. It is rather like they do on Star Ship Enterprise, 'Beam me up Scotty'."

Father Christmas assured the Captain that the suit would keep his companion warm. "No sweat," or rather he would sweat, he would sweat quite a lot. But he was still not sure that this beam thing could really do what the Captain said it would.

The Captain was becoming convinced that Father Christmas was genuine and made another offer, "We can give you a portable Zapper to take with you. It will Zap the toys into the houses without you having to go scraping down the chimneys, but it only works for short distances."

Father Christmas was even more delighted and the portable Zapper was fixed to his sleigh. It looked like a cross between a microwave and a search light. You had to put the package into the back of the thing just as you would put something into a microwave and there was a beam of green light from the other side. The label on the present was scanned; and, just like Google Earth or a 'Sat Nav,' can find any house, the beam of light was automatically pointed at the house; after fingers typed the address on a key board; a final button was pressed and the package was zapped down the beam and into the house.

They set off in the sleigh and after half an hour of Zapping the alien contacted his base ship to say that he was still warm and he was comfortable in his suit. He received a message back to say that since the suit was working, the Zapping aboard the space ship would start.

Even though Father Christmas had been delayed the toys were all delivered without having to get down a single chimney.

When Father Christmas took the alien back to the space ship, the Captain said he would have a lot to write in his log book, about all humans not being greedy and how at least one of them did good deeds and helped others for free. He said he would give Father Christmas the portable Zapper as a present from him.

He said, "Owing to the cold he had not discovered this present-giving season among humans."

That is why Father Christmas does not now need you to leave your door unlocked and he is not bothered if there is no chimney to your house. He can deliver all the toys with his new Zapper right into your bedroom.

But, but, if, some winter's day you see a man wearing an airman's suit walking about town, he may be a friend of Father Christmas and he may be an alien, but I am sure he won't be wishing any of us any harm. He will probably be collecting his statistical information about us humans. He will be making a list of how many of us are kind and generous to others and how many are selfish and greedy. See that your name is included with Father Christmas in the 'kind' column'.

*   *   *

MY SPACE

I have a place, an Aladdin's Cave,
It's my space where I can rant and rave.
I wouldn't mind if it were my grave,
I can visit there and need not shave.

Though it looks just like a souk Bazaar,
You may consider me "kook," bizarre.
But within its walls I am a Czar,
With my kingdom reaching near and far.

I tinker about mending this and that,
With many great ideas, some fall flat.
But must warn you in a caveat,
There may be some stuff, like Paraquat.

There's an old glue pot in small carrel,
Which, when in use has a pungent smell.
Its looks, to put it in a nut shell,
It's black, as black as the hobs of hell.

From household chores I am an abstainer,
For equal rights I am a campaigner.
While her indoors my dear Czarina,
Clocks miles and miles on her vacuum cleaner.

She's often got a flea in her ear,
Saying words like work, that I dread and fear.
You can guess to where I disappear,
Returning only when the coast is clear.

*   *   *

BASMA AL-HUSSEIN

Basma Al-Hussein was the daughter of a Sultana,
She was sure she would one day, win at a Gymkhana.
She rode her pony all day long and he got very tired,
She rode it once too often, and her pony, it expired.

Mrs Jones was bending over a large cardboard box which contained all manner of bric-a-brac. You could hear the clatter of porcelain and glass as she selected the items in the order which she considered to be of greatest value or attraction. After dusting each one she placed them on the counter in groups, crockery into one group, vases and ornaments in another. A windmill with attached hour glass, probably some child's present to Grandma from some holiday, was discarded. She was so engrossed in her task of itemising the articles that she did not, for a long time, notice the young girl anxiously waiting in the shop doorway.

Mrs Jones eventually stood up to ease her aching back, and in so doing turned and saw a little girl. She was a very young girl, of about eight years, with long blonde plaits. She was hovering from one foot to the other hesitantly.

"Hello," said Mrs Jones as she brushed her hair back from her eyes. "What can I do for you? You're too young for our sort of help, so what do you want to buy? Taken a fancy to the teddy in the window have you?"

The young girl shifted from one foot to the other while summoning up courage to speak, then she blurted out, "No, I don't want to buy anything, but what do I have to bring to get help for my Granddad?"

Mrs Jones smiled kindly and asked, "What kind of help would you be wanting?"

"I don't know," said the little girl. "But I want someone to make his dinners."

"I have an idea," said Mrs Jones, "why don't you first tell me your name? Then we can talk about how we may be able to help your Granddad."

The smile relaxed the young girl who, gaining courage, burst forth with, "My name is Mary, and my Grandma died, and my Granddad lives by himself and doesn't know how to cook and Mummy takes dinners to him, and she sometimes comes home late from work and Granddad is very hungry before then."

"It sounds as though this Granddad of yours needs lots and lots of help from us. How old is your Granddad?" asked Mrs Jones.

"Eighty-three," said Mary.

"Well now, that's plenty old enough to be helped by us. That's what we do here at 'Help the Aged'. We help old Granddads."

In spite of the reassuring smile, Mary persisted. "What do I have to bring? Will a wheelbarrow, a spade and a fork do? I've got Granddad's outside," she said anxiously, "He doesn't use them now."

Giving her reassuring smile again Mrs Jones replied, "Well, Miss Mary, we have never had a barrow full of gardening tools before, but I'm sure they will be sufficient to get your Granddad some help, in fact all the help he needs." Then turning to the counter, she picked up a pen and made to write in a big book.

"Now Miss Mary, what is your Granddad's name and what is his address?"

Mrs Jones wrote down all the information Mary had given, then she assured Mary by saying, "Now I have a lot of information about your Granddad, and tomorrow morning one of our helpers will call around to your Granddad." But she said, "Before you run off home with this good news you will have to help me to get this barrow into the shop."

Next day Granddad was alone in his house when a nice lady called on him. Introducing herself she said, "Hello, you must be Mr Taylor. I have come from 'Help the Aged,' I'm Elizabeth, but just call me Betty. Your granddaughter Mary, a very bright little girl, is worried about you and insists that you need some help."

She asked Granddad a lot of questions about whether he could hold the kettle and if he could make himself a cup of tea, how long has he needed to use his walking stick, could he wash himself, and how does he do his washing?

The next day Mary could not wait to see the help that her Granddad had been promised. She thought about it all day and as soon as she was free from school she rushed around to Granddad's house. Granddad related to her all that he could remember. How 'Betty' wrote lots of things in her notebook, and helped him fill in some forms and said she would have to meet Mum. Mary was very disappointed. It sounded as though this Betty had been very nice, but she hadn't brought any help and she didn't say what help she would bring.

A few days later, Mary was with her Granddad, when Betty returned with another lady.

Betty said, "You must be Mary who asked for our help. Well, we will get him some help. I have brought a lady from Social Services to see what we do can for him."

This other lady looked very important with her briefcase filled with forms. She wore glasses and while she thought and asked questions, she kept removing them and chewing the end of the arm. She asked Granddad lots of questions about dinners, banks and pensions books. How often Mum cooked for him, when did he go to the doctor, how long was it since Grandma died? It all seemed pointless to Mary, who did not know what Social Service meant and why couldn't they couldn't understand that granddad needed help with his dinners.

Granddad told her that he only had his old-age pension, which was less than when Martha had been alive, although as he said, "The electricity, gas and the rates cost just the same as they did before." He could but only with difficulty wash and shave himself, because he had rheumatism and he couldn't see very well. He explained that Rachael, his daughter, did for him when she could, but she had a full-time job at Tesco's. He could make tea, but he was living on sandwiches. He got a hot dinner, only, when Rachael could manage it.

Granddad seemed confused, but Betty helped him to answer all the questions, and after a long time, the lady put all the papers into her briefcase and left. She did not say she would get help or when she would come back.

Betty stayed to make some tea for the three of them. Afterwards, while Betty and Mary washed the cups, Betty confided her hopes to Mary. "We think we can get Granddad some help. It is called, 'Income Support'," she said, "that's, sort of, more pension."

"But," said Mary, "he still won't be able to cook."

Betty explained, "If your Granddad gets some extra money, I can arrange for meals, like dinner, to be brought to him when your Mum can't. Then your Granddad won't be waiting for your Mum to come home from work." She went on, "There might be enough to pay a cleaning lady to come and do some cleaning for him."

This sounded like really good news to Mary.

"But," cautioned Betty, "we must first talk to your Mum about it, she will need to fill in a lot of forms."

It was a week and a bit before the brief-case lady came to see

Mum, because Mum could not get off work during the day. Mary had begun to think that Granddad was never going to get some help, and it was summer holidays before Granddad did get some help.

One day, during school holidays, Mary was with her Granddad when there was a 'rat-a tat tat tat' on the door.

"That'll be Mrs Murphy, my new cleaning lady," said Granddad, "She always makes that noise on the door. She must think I'm deaf. Will you go and let her in please Mary."

Mrs Murphy, a rather rotund lady with a wrap around pinafore, was talking from the minute she crossed the threshold. She struggled through the door with her brushes, dusters and mop; walked straight to the kitchen where she deposited the tools of her trade, and hung up her coat. All this was done while saying, "How are you today Mr Taylor? Had any more backache? See you have new specs. So this must be Mary, the granddaughter you were telling me about. She's a fine looking girl and obviously clever too. Can you make tea dearie?"

Mrs Murphy set to work while Mary set the cups for the tea. The buckets, brushes and mop could not have moved faster even if directed by the sorcerer's apprentice. The vacuum cleaner whirred into action putting many miles on its clock. Mary watched and listened as the simultaneous cleaning and conversation continued. "I see your garden is looking smart. That gardener hasn't wasted any time in getting it sorted. How often does he come?" Mrs Murphy talked and asked questions, but never seemed to listen or be interested in the answers.

It did not seem long before Mrs Murphy said, "Ten minutes and we will have some tea, how about it Mary?"

Mary carefully filled the kettle and switched it on to boil in the way Granddad had taught her. When the tea was ready, Mrs Murphy went out to her car and brought in a home-baked, cream sponge cake with glace cherries on the top. "Your Granddad said you would be here today and he told me that it is your birthday and you are nine, so I made this cake for us to have a party for elevenses."

The cake was delicious. Mary thanked Mrs Murphy for it and asked could she take the last of the cake to her mother? With the wish granted, Mrs Murphy washed and dried the dishes that they had used and went on her way. Still talking as she left the house. "Oh! I'll have to clean this porch next time I come."

Mary had noticed that someone had been doing the garden and asked Granddad about it.

"Oh!" said Granddad. "I have to pay the gardener man. He only comes once a week, on Tuesdays for two hours, but I'm now getting extra money in my pension so I can afford it."

Later there was another knock on the door, a gentler one.

"That will be the 'Meals on Wheels' people," said Granddad, "Go and open the door for them, but just you wait till you see what I get. Yesterday it was roast beef and roastie potatoes."

Mary opened the door to a red faced man who had also been apprised of Mary's request for help.

He opened with, "Hello, are you the Mary we have all been talking about? I've heard all about you. Hello! Mr Taylor, the dinner is, 'foul' today."

Mary was puzzled. Did he mean the dinner was awful?

Noting the expression on her face he said "Roast chicken, that's fowl isn't it?" then he burst out laughing at his joke.

"Quick Mary," said Granddad, "get the mat for the table, it will be very hot."

Mary placed the heat mat under the hot tray, saying, "It smells lovely, and look! There's an apple pie as well."

As the dinner man left he said to Granddad, "Lucky Granddad at 'Chinese toothache time,' you know, 'Tooth hurty,' for the two-thirty," and he again laughed at his own joke.

Granddad thanked the dinner gentleman but Mary did not understand the Tooth hurty.

Granddad explained that the dinner man was always making jokes and must have thought that he, Granddad, was a gambler on horses. "He was trying to tell me that there is a horse called, 'Lucky Granddad,' in some race or other at half past two, 'Two-thirty,' but it might be just his way of making a joke." Mary set the table with the knives, forks, cups, etc. and put the kettle on, then sat down to open the cheese sandwiches that her mum had made for her. Granddad was tucking into his 'foul' chicken.

"Is that dinner as nice as it smells?" Mary asked.

"Yes it is, very," said Granddad, "And you can tell your Mum that I ate all my greens."

Mary was impressed and asked, "Is it always as nice?"

"Yes," said granddad, "but today I've saved some of the apple pie for you. It's delicious."

As Mary ate the pie she said, I'll have to tell Mum about this pie. She never has time to bake pies these days.

Granddad consoled her, "Your Mum and your Grandma used to bake a lot of nice cakes and pies, like the one Mrs Murphy baked and brought today. Maybe your mum will have more time now that she does not have to do so much for me."

Mary lapsed into a sort of trance, as if she were chewing the cud, and with a thoughtful look on her face slowly said, "Granddad."

"Yes dear?" said Granddad, indicating that he was all ears.

"I was just thinking."

"What were you just thinking?"

"I was thinking."

"Yes."

"I was thinking,—don't you get a lot of help for an old barrow, a spade and a fork?"

*   *   *

MAGIC WORDS

That you should start or end with an endearing word,
Is sound advice, though it seems absurd.
If you take this advice to its extreme,
You can shout and you can even scream.
But if you end with love or dear,
All aggressive thought will disappear.
When blood is boiling and the air is blue,
Heed these words you'll find them true.
Just slip in an endearing word,
Above all others that one will be heard.
Any like honey, darling, love, will do,
It will reconcile both points of view.

*   *   *

THE FAIRY CONCERT

You won't believe this, but one bright spring moonlit night, sometime about 1945, I was in my shed at the bottom of the garden. It was my dark room where I develop photographs. I often went there at night. I must have been there for an hour or more when I heard the sound of tinkling bells and flutes. I looked through a knot hole in the boards and saw twinkling lights. I thought, "Fairies?"

Fairies in their dozens were assembling. I stayed very quiet in my shed and realised that it was an orchestra assembling. They were all very excited, plink plonking and tootle fluting, tuning their instruments. I did not know it at first, but they were there to practise for a Royal Command Performance in front of their Fairy Queen.

From my secret hideout in the shed I could not see too well, even though it was a bright moonlit night. I had to be very, very still but I could see that some of their dresses looked as though they were made of crocus petals and some of daffodil petals.

There was a harpist making music on her spider web harp. The spider was most disconcerted; he didn't seem to like it at all. There was a rather feisty timpani-playing fairy, beating out her music on her various toadstools drums. Another one of the percussion group was beating, as if on a bass drum, but on the sides of a large snail. The snail did not seem to mind but waved its antenna in time with the music. There was another which I had difficulty seeing through the cracks in the boards. She was intent on tuning up an instrument like a cello. But it was an upturned crocus. The head of the crocus was between her knees, her bow was of a grass stalk and spider silk.

There were players of the blue-bells as a sort of vertical xylophone. There were even sweeter sounds from the hare-bells and there was a great bell-ringing tintinnabulation coming from the hyacinth. Wind instruments were of hollow grass stalks of various thicknesses. There were flutes and oboes. Did you never make pan pipes from straws when you were at school? But those making the loudest music were the horns. And the most interesting of these were the tuba-sounding daffodils.

Now, unbeknown to the fairies and to me, there was another eavesdropping on their rehearsal. There was a bullfrog hiding in the grass, he had also been keeping quiet and listening intently.

More and more fairies without instruments came and sat around on tufts of sheep wool, the sort of tufts that you find clinging to barbed wire where sheep have grazed. I thought that these fairies might have been members of a choir. The stars on their many wands were twinkling in the moonlight. Presently the musicians' instruments were tuned to their satisfaction and all gradually went quiet. It was then that a most beautiful fairy made an entrance and all the fairies stood up. She signalled to them with her wand to be seated. She leaned her wand against the rostrum and picked up an anther baton that was lying on the many pages of music that were on the rostrum. It was then that I realised she was their conductor. She was dressed in tulip petals making a rather sticky-out skirt. She spoke in a voice that I could hear clearly, "Now fairies, I want you to practise hard because we want the Queen, when she hears our music, to think that it is the best performance she has ever heard." She continued, "You all have the programme and your music in order I hope?"

Lots of heads nodded in agreement. Then she called them to order and raised her anther baton to signal the downbeat.

They played, to my mind magnificently, but the fairy conductor was often not happy with the sound and had them go over and over some parts. The music and the melodies were so beautiful that it was quite hypnotic. I found my feet tapping and had to stop them in case they were heard, but my feet were difficult to control.

There was a particular melody played by the daffodil-tubas. It was in a very low register. The conductor was not happy with their efforts. She seemed not happy at all and said, "Come on daffodils you can do better than that." They played and replayed it several times over until she was happy with them. With a word of encouragement she praised them saying, "That was excellent, play it like that on the night and we will all be happy. Now once again, everybody, from bar seventeen."

Of course I cannot describe this beautiful music without an orchestra or at least a tuba so you must imagine it but the bullfrog must have been overcome with the hypnotic music and even I could hear him humming along with the enchanting fairy music. The conductor on hearing the frog became angry and rapped her baton on the rostrum indicating that they should all be silent. It was then that, in an otherwise still night, the bullfrog's singing could be clearly heard. "Bur, bur-b-bur, bur-b-b-bur, b-b-bur-b-b-bur-b-b-bur,"

Immediately there was a state of turmoil among the fairies. It seemed as though they might have lynched the bullfrog but fairies do not do such terrible things. However they were certainly very annoyed, fluttering about like a swarm of bees. The bullfrog quickly came out of his trance and hopped off as fast as he could, which was much faster than the fairies could fly.

I could hear many conversations all quoting the lore of fairy music. This seemed to say that the scores of fairy music were secret, to be kept in fairyland and performed only by fairies. If some other musician played any of it, then fairies were never again to use that particular piece of music in their repertoires.

In the distance the bullfrog could be heard singing the fairy melody at the top of his voice, "Bur, bur-b-bur, bur-b-b-bur, b-b-bur-b-b-bur-b-b-bur" The fairy daffodil tuba players had found it so difficult, and so they were beside themselves with grief. There were not very many melodies which were written specifically for their type of instrument. I made a vow there and then that I would not hum or convey any of the melodies that I had heard to anybody in case I caused the fairies to discard whole passages of their ensorceling music.

Right outside the shed there was a conversation which I could hear clearly. It related to a very sad story. It seemed that a very long time ago, there had been a man named Tchaikovsky who captured a fairy. He placed her in a box and held her captive. The fairy was called Sugar Plum and was a very accomplished dancer. She thought that if she sang her song from inside the box, other fairies would hear it and, knowing it to be a fairy song, would make attempts to rescue her. However before the fairy was rescued the man also heard the song and wrote down every note. Lots of humans now play the song of the Sugar Plum Fairy and others try their 'legs' at dancing to it, but I am sure that none can perform as well as the seemingly famous fairy dancer, Sugar Plum. Perhaps you have heard the tune? The fairies did rescue her but the cost of rescuing her was that she and all other fairies had to discard her song forever.

The fairies were eventually consoled by the conductor who thought it best to cancel the rehearsal for that night because a new programme was needed. Slowly they all dispersed, some still sobbing, especially the tuba players.

I went to the shed the next night, but I did not see or hear a rehearsal. It may be that they chose a more secluded place to practise and perform. But since then I have often looked through the crack in the shed and seen some fairies, not an orchestra, so I know they still live near. I do hope that a fairy has written a new, equally beautiful, melody to replace the one stolen from them.

Years later after the frog had stolen the Fairies' Daffodil—tuba melody; I heard a strange story of a man named Danny Kaye who was an actor. He lived in America and was so famous that the Queen had commanded him to performing, in England at the famous Palladium Theatre in London. He later told a story of a young human tuba player sitting on the river bank in the moonlight. The boy was very, very unhappy because, like the daffodil tuba players, he very seldom had a melody to play. To add to his sadness that very afternoon Señor Pizzicato, the famous conductor, had been rehearsing the orchestra in the famous Albert Hall, and the boy tuba player had played a wrong note. Señor Pizzicato had been very cross

The boy was so unhappy that he was about to throw his tuba in the river when he heard a bullfrog singing a wonderful tune, "Bur, bur-b-bur, bur-b-b-bur, b-b-bur-b-b-bur-b-b-bur," It sounded so beautiful that one could swear it had been written especially for tubas. The boy practised it and practised it until he could play it perfectly. He then rushed back to the concert hall to find that the orchestra were reassembling after a coffee break. He gave an impromptu performance to the other members of his orchestra, "Bur, bur-b-bur, bur-b-b-bur, b-b-bur-b-b-bur-b-b-bur,"

Señor Pizzicato said, "I've never heard a tuba play a melody before," and all the orchestra went in raptures about this fine tuba melody. Such was the commotion that the violins were twitching their strings in excitement; the percussion was beating its heart out. The piccolos, flutes, oboes and clarinets were quite out of breath. Everyone wanted to play the melody.

Now I don't think it could be the same bullfrog; maybe my frog taught it to lots of other frogs. But this American man, Mr Danny Kaye, took the tune back to America and made it very famous. As I have said, Mr Kaye was a very famous man and the tune was exactly the same so I believe him. And the rest, as they say, is history.

HARRIET

It almost makes me sad to tell,
What foolish Harriet befell.
She had been told time and again,
From drugs and alcohol, refrain.
To mum's advice she would not heed,
With every word she disagreed.
Mum claimed her friends were not too nice,
She should have thought about them twice.
But Harriet, she knew better,
Freed herself from mother's fetter.
Insisting they are decent types,
When they were really gutter snipes.
A glass of this will do no harm,
The cockles of your heart will warm.
A slug of this and you'll feel good,
A claim that she should have withstood.
Some things they did were super cool,
With contents from a glass ampoule.
As time went by she paid the price,
Of having friends who are not nice.
Many times, she was heard to say,
For one fix you can have your way.
Heed my words and remember well,
How Harriet came to the gates of hell.
For Harriet there was no hope,
A slave to a seller of dope to a dope.

*   *   *

"Ladies and gentlemen, you have five hours to explore Llangollen. Will you please be back on the bus at five o-clock." The bus driver was giving his routine instructions to the day trippers on his coach. "You can take a walk along the river, take a barge along the canal, ride on the steam train to Glyndyfrdwy or, if you feel really energetic, climb to the castle ruins."

His passengers were all, but for two, Senior Citizens who were most unlikely to be going up to the castle ruins. The two juniors were a young couple, John and Anne, both in their early twenties. Married for two years, they were obviously still very happy to be so. As each passenger stepped down from the coach the driver monotonously said to each, "Have a nice day."

Anne had been to Llangollen many years before, when she was a ten year old Girl Guide. Now, as they left the coach park, she had a touch of dé já vu. As she stopped on the bridge to look into the river and take in the wonderful view of mountains, the sun was reflecting on the rippling water giving the appearance of shoals of surfacing silver fish.

They walked up a steep hill towards a sign which read, 'Café and Boat Rides'. At the café on the wharf they ordered tea and cakes while they watched a magnificent shire horse pull a boatload of children along the canal.

"I am sure the campsite was up that hill," said Anne, as she pointed to a narrow road with a sign pointing to the castle.

"What campsite was this?" said John.

"Oh!" she said, "I was here years ago with the Guides. I am sure we camped somewhere up there."

"Let's see if we can find it," said John, "we have plenty of time."

"If it is the hill, it is very steep," she said, "it was nothing when I was ten, but I don't know if I am up to it now that I am an old married woman."

"Come on," John said as picked up their bag of victuals "if you can't find the site, the view from the castle must be worth the effort."

It was a stiff climb, with every field being assessed for its fauna and flora until, on the left near a farm she declared, "This is it but it is so small, I remember it as a huge acreage." She tried to remember and describe the camp, recalling some of the songs they sang, one in particular about eating worms.

Surveying the landscape she said, "We went on a treasure hunt up that hill and along that ledge up there."

"What kind of treasure hunt? How long did it take you to get up there?"

"About half an hour," She said and added. "We had special secret signs, or we thought them very secret, known only to Guides and Scouts."

John whispered in her ear, "Were they too secret to tell me?"

"I could be compromised if you parted with a kiss," she replied.

"A bargain," he said, as he grabbed her in his arms giving her a hug and the desired kiss.

"Well," she pondered, "that has earned you the details of one, and there are about twenty."

She explained that arrows and other signs, made of any natural material were made on the floor, under seats or stiles, on trees, walls or anywhere. You have to look carefully to find them." She arranged some small stones in lines making an 'X' saying, "An 'X' in any material like this, means don't go this way."

As he pulled her further up the hill he said, "Let's go and see if there are any still out there."

"I remember this wooden fence but it had new bright green paint then, and there is a stile somewhere up there on the right," Anne said, as she speeded up, eager to find it, "there was an arrow sign under it then."

John overtook her to find the stile, but alas there was no arrow sign.

Over the stile, into a field, down a valley and, at a plank bridge across a stream Anne jumped for joy. There were eleven big white stones, rough, but as big as footballs, arranged in echelon formation. It clearly made the bridge into the staff of an arrow. Excitement spurred them on, up a field out of the valley.

Jumpers came off and were tied around waists. They reached another stile beyond which was a narrow road and open rising moor.

"I remember two big stone crosses with an arrow in the centre," she puffed, as she sat on the stile, "somewhere on that side of the road."

There were a lot of large stones, but none placed to form an arrow. They could have been the arrow. They would not have needed much effort to have placed them to form an arrow. The path went upwards and over the moor. It reached the track of an old mineral railway which had been cut into the face of the cliff.

"Turn left here," Anne said with confidence, "there is a fantastic view from just along there and it's even higher than the castle."

They dawdled along this ledge taking in the stupendous view. At a break in the cliff face they sat on a grassy slope, to eat and admire the wonderful view of the castle and the Vale of Llangollen.

Anne told of another memory that came flooding back. "Somewhere here, there was an arrow attached to a square," she said, making shapes with her finger, "in the square there were some stones denoting the number of paces from the square to a secret message which had to be found."

"Do you mean here or further along there?" John questioned.

She pointed further along the path, "It has to be somewhere along there."

Putting the box of sandwiches back in the bag he suggested that they move on to find the spot.

"It was obvious where the real message was hidden," she told him, "it pointed to hollow tree."

John pondered, "Then we must find a hollow tree, a tree cannot disappear."

The track entered a flat area where there was a fallen tree. "Could this be it?" John asked her, and settled to sit with his back to the tree and resume his lunch. Anne sat on the grass opposite him scanning the trunk and bole for a sign that it had been hollow.

John finished his sandwiches and asked, "What was the message, did you find it in the tree?"

Yes she said, "A note, read, 'Take one bar of chocolate and one bottle of lemonade per group, put the message back and quickly move on your way'."

"Were you all together in one group or were there other groups following on?"

"We were in patrols but there was a terrible thunder storm.

The leaders came to collect us. One patrol never got their goodies."

"So," said John, "it is likely that there is still a bottle of lemonade in this tree?"

"Quite likely," said Anne, "our Guide Captain gave them a bottle and chocolate in camp, while we dried our clothes."

Anne then had a sudden reflection, not about the treasure, "You haven't paid the fee for all this information about our Guide secrets."

He leaned forward from a sitting position against the tree and pushed her back on the grass. Pinning her down he rained kiss after kiss after kiss on her lips, then just held her and hugged her.

They lay there for a minute or two before she said, "The secrets of our guides are worth a lot more than that, but if that was just a down payment?"

His lips stopped anymore demands and all conversation ceased.

Eventually, Anne came up for air and spoke in a whisper, "I hate to mention this now that I have succumbed to your charm and compromised all of the Guide Association's secrets but, if you find any treasure, the charges will be double."

"In that case, I can't wait to find the hollow in this tree, but I must say, you drive a hard bargain."

He moved around the bole to the exposed roots.

"No sign of it being hollow here," he said.

Moving to the farthest side of the tree, he called her to see a large hole in the trunk, "Is this the hollow?"

"Yes, quick, see if there is anything inside." She said excitedly, but he was already rolling up his sleeve.

"Oh! Sh. . . . ," he said as he drew his arm back out, "it's full of mush and rubbish." He wiped his hand on the tree trunk and then on the grass.

"Get your hand back in that muck," she said, moving away as if not to get contaminated, "It might come out covered in diamonds or money. You know what they say, where there's muck there's money."

"You mean, I might be luckier than I am already?" He screwed his nose up as he contemplated the remaining grunge on his hand.

"What do you mean you might get luckier than you are

already?"

"Well," he said dryly, "I have this big debt to you hanging over me like the sword of Damocles, and if that isn't lucky?"

"You had better get your hand back in there before your luck runs out!" Her voice was commanding.

"Yes ma'am," he said, with a salute and thrust his arm into the gunge filled hole.

There was a lot of heaving and stretching. "There is something here and it doesn't feel like a bottle." He pulled his hand out and rubbed a glass jar on the grass trying to avoid getting his other hand contaminated.

"It's a screw topped jam jar," and his clean hand instinctively tried to unscrew the top.

"Yes," Anne said, "the chocolate bars were in a jar, are there any inside?"

He tipped the jar to empty any contents onto the grass and out fell a bar of Cadbury's chocolate. The wrapper was somewhat mouldy. "I think it's past the sell by date," he said, as he poked it with his dirty finger, "does it count as treasure?"

"Definitely does," said Anne, as she pointed to the hole and gestured to try again for the bottle.

Feigning his wish to disobey, he said, "Do I have to?"

"What sort of a man are you to be afraid of a few beetles and rotten tree trunk?" she sneered. "We guides were dared to pick up worms and all sorts of bugs, spiders and even mice."

He again pretended to resist, but reached into the tree again and after a bit of rummaging and pretending that his arm had become stuck in the hole, he brought out a plastic lemonade bottle. It was lumpy like a large potato, but it was a lemonade bottle. They could read on the mouldy label, 'White's Lemonade.' He placed it on the ground and wiped his arm and hands with some paper handkerchiefs from Anne's handbag.

Anne ruminated, "That bottle and chocolate have been in that tree all this time."

As he rolled his sleeve down John said, "The lemonade has been frozen a few times. Frozen liquids expand, that would account for the funny shape of the plastic now."

Anne took his hand and with her linen handkerchief tried to clean between his fingers. She said, "It too is well past its sell by date, but it's a pity it's not wine, it would have matured and been just the thing we need for our celebration."

"Celebrate what?" John asked.

"Oh," said Anne, pulling him by the hand until she could kiss him, "We need to celebrate, because we are going to have a Brownie that we can send to camp."

*   *   *

HEAD IN THE AIR:
FEET ON THE GROUND

Harry would not do his lessons, football was all he'd learn,
Every day he thought about the money he would earn.
He'd be an international, and live a life like Beck's,
But if he cannot read or write, how will he sign his cheques?

Scoring the goals with head or foot, fans would love him dearly.
He was sure that come his time, he'd play in Europe yearly.
He'd have a car, Mercedes Benz, and things all given free,
He would never need to get a bachelor's degree.

He wouldn't need Geography, he'd need the off-side rule,
He thought it oh so stupid, to spend the day at school.
He's sure the ways of foreigners, won't bother him too much,
But when they play Juventus, are they French or are they Dutch?

Foreign language that's a bore, who'd want to speak in German?
Legs are moved and not your lips, to score like Deitmar Hamann.
Who knows what the fates decide, it may cost him quite dearly,
If reasons for a yellow card, are given in Swahili.

Science is not a thing he'll need; it's not used to score a goal,
It never seems to cross his mind, that he may need the dole.
It matters not how well you play, you still need lots of schooling,
If he thinks it otherwise, it's himself that he is fooling.

*   *   *

Situated at the foot of the Dolomites and bathed by the warm Mediterranean climate are the Italian Lakes of Garda, Maggiore and Como. Como, with its dreamy quality, is arguably the most beautiful of these three lakes. It is a place of outstanding beauty with its ferry boats skimming their criss-cross paths across otherwise placid water, with a backdrop of rocky promontories against towering pine-clad mountains. Here and there one can pick out picturesque villages along the shoreline. Villages which have, for centuries, inspired generations of writers, artists and scientists, among whom was Verdi and a physicist named Volta.

Tremezzo is one of those villages nestling on the shore where there is a Hotel Balionie. The Hotel Balionie has its feet in the lake, there being a piazza or veranda, supported on piles reaching over the lake. The hotel commands a panoramic view of the lake which surpasses that of any other hotel in Tremezzo. Alas, this hotel does not boast a galaxy of stars and in consequence does not attract the 'Grand Tour' type of client, but attracts, for the most part, British tourists of the budget class.

Apart from the Owner-Manager the staff were mostly itinerants being employed for only one season. There was a custodian of the bar, who called herself a manager, but who was more like a barmaid. She claimed that in England she had been a manageress of a restaurant. Her demeanour belied such a claim, unless it was the 'Greasy Spoon,' the transport café on the A34. She was always over-painted, had a penchant for bawdy stories and invading the male client's' body-space. These attributes, together with a raucous laugh, helped to make her insufferably cheerful. Nevertheless, the receipts of the bar were presumably acceptable to the owner.

There were eleven waiters, well, ten people who took food to tables, seven of whom were local Italian, two German, one English student and one English man of senior years. This English man had an impeccable pedigree. He had learnt his craft from the age of 14, in the days when the L.M.S. Railway had high-class, palatial hotels adjacent to every main-line station in the British Isles. Gleneagles in Scotland had been one of them. He mourned the passing of such hotels into the private sector when it was said that they would improve. He had been made redundant and was supplementing his meagre pension with seedy employment in sunny climates.

A large English girl, Evelyn, of about 19 years, with an ample bosom, was a waitress. Her hair was an outrageous confection of candyfloss. Her smile revealed two rows of perfect white teeth. She was a student of Cardiff University, studying Art & Design, and was overjoyed to have found employment in an area steeped in the arts. Her burning desire was to immerse herself in all manner of the arts which now surrounded her. This included everything from the Renaissance to date. To this end, she intended to please and be good at this job in the hope that she could return again during her recessions. She was teamed with the English waiter. Milan is only half an hour drive away from Como and on Saturdays and Sundays there is an influx of trippers from the great city. The Hotel Balionie was very busy on these days with all tables, even on the terrace, in constant occupation. At the bar there was usually much laughter and wine drinking, sometimes to the chagrin of those diners out on the terrace who required alcoholic refreshment with their meal. The owner busied himself as Maitre d'. It was on just such a day that we arrived, in the late afternoon, to spend our two weeks holiday at Lake Como. As resident guests, when we went down to dinner in the early evening, the day trippers were then heading back to Milan and the rush was over. The Maitre d' welcomed us and escorted us to a window table with a waterfront view.

The tall waiter drew our attention from the moment we stepped into the dining room, even before we had been shown to our seats. He walked with an almost military bearing, but with slower and shorter paces. His silver-grey hair and white moustache gave away his years. The dark suit was no schlock, definitely bespoken, with gleaming white shirt and a tie which matched his hair. In one hand he carried a napkin or towel. His shoes, though worn, were highly polished. He instantly noticed, although the Maitre d' did not, that, although we were seated at a table with a glorious view, the sun was making me squint.

"Would madam prefer to be seated at another table?" he enquired.

As we settled ourselves at his recommended table, still with a lakeside view, I noticed him adjust some of the cutlery into, what was to his eye, a perfect position, before handing each of us a menu.

While his hands were occupied he would place the napkin neatly across his arm.

"Would madam like something to drink? And you sir?"

While we deliberated for a second or two he scanned the other guests in his sector and ensured that his protégée was busy serving soup. He noticeably moved the napkin from his arm to his hand. One of the guests required his attention and with a half salute he signalled that he would soon be in attendance. He mentally recorded our choice of drinks and proceeded to the other guest. Some conversation took place then he went to remove used dishes from another guest's table, the napkin was now neatly on his arm. I watched in fascination as the napkin moved from hand to arm and back, without losing its crisp, neatly folded form, obviously the result of many years of practice. As he left the room laden with dishes he again scanned all the guests, not just those on his allotted tables, this time gesturing with his head that he acknowledged someone's need. As the week went by we could see the professional influence he was having on Evelyn's performance as a waitress. Never did she go to the kitchen empty-handed or without casting an eye over the diners in case they should require some service.

This was in contrast to the other so-called waiters, who seemed to have tunnel vision. When serving a table, they did it in total oblivion of all else around them. Other tables or guests may not have existed. Serve one table at a time, bring the dessert and then clear the main-dish crockery. If cutlery was missing from a poorly laid table it was impossible to attract their attention. There was no apology when a guest, having waited almost until their meal was cold, helped themselves to the required cutlery. We were much pleased, educated and enchanted with the efficiency of our waiter.

Later in the evening, having retired to the lounge we could assess some of the other resident guests and play guessing games as to who and what their occupation might be. There were several men of various ages on bar stools being entertained by, 'Ms. Manageress of the Bar,' and spasms of hearty laughter emanated there-from. There was a retired couple, obviously British, reticent and overawed with their surroundings. I had noticed them at dinner, the waiter, our waiter, had spent a lot of time at their table, probably interpreting the menu. They sat in a corner seat of the lounge; she was now enjoying her Bacardi and Coke: he his lager.

Sitting on her own, with two empty glasses at her side, was a very finely-clad lady who wore an exceptionally well-cut trouser or safari suit of the palest of yellow, the jacket of which was draped over the adjacent chair. While she took occasional sips of her third Martini, she was engrossed in some sort of document or letter, and seemed to be making copious notes.

Initially, sitting on his own, was a man pouring over a map. He had a rosy outdoor complexion. After a while he folded his map, picked up his whisky and moved to join the elderly couple. He had been out hiking and was eager to tell them, in his loud broad Yorkshire accent, about his exploits. The couple were only too glad to have someone to make conversation. They were the epitome of, 'W.S. Gilbert's' advice on etiquette, 'don't speak until you are spoken to.'

After a sixth Martini the well-groomed lady decided to retire, but on leaving she left her jacket on the chair. I picked it up and followed her unsteady steps to the lift. As I passed it to her, I observed the makers label.

YVES SAINT LAURENT.

COUTURE.

5 AVENUE MARCAU.

PARIS.

I mused that, if it were genuine, this lady was slumming in the Hotel Balionie.

She thanked me profusely and said, "I owe you a drink, but I have had enough for tonight, maybe tomorrow."

I said, "That will be the easiest drink I have ever earned,"

While her feet were unsure her brain was obviously not, she gave a smart rejoinder. "A simple coat gesture earned Walter Raleigh a knighthood. See you tomorrow. Thanks again and goodnight."

At breakfast the lady, who had dined alone, preferred not to breakfast on her own, came and asked our permission to sit at our table. Hardly had she sat down than the waiter, with his usual efficiency, hastily set the place for her. She and the waiter proffered advice on where and what we should visit. He was a mine of information. Neglecting their advice for our first day we spent the morning in and around Tremezzo, watching people who were, 'Just messing about in boats'. There were hundreds of them.

By the time of our fifth day we had settled to a routine. We had observed that others also had their routines. After breakfast had been cleared and tables set for lunch, the waiter would change to mufti, seek a corner of the terrace, and read his English newspaper until lunch time.

The student waitress, when she was off duty, was even more outrageous in her dress. She sometimes wore a studded dog-collar necklace and, despite the climate, thigh length leather boots and all-black dresses.

The sundry men, usually at the bar, would laze in the sun on a lower patio, be brought drinks by the 'Bar Manager', now and then there would be peals of laughter and, if the mood took them, swim.

'Thar-Knows' from Yorkshire went walking with his haversack and packed lunch, often meeting up with other like-minded holiday-makers from other hotels. Every night he would pour over his maps, we assumed he was tracing the route on which he had been led that day. We also supposed that he was mentally reconnoitring for the following day. He would then move to the company of 'Derby and Joan" for the rest of the evening.

'Derby and Joan', always took the waiter's advice. They took arranged trips, or ventured on public transport along the lakeside. They were most confident on the ferries.

'Sophisticated Lady,' breakfasted and dined with us, and spent her mornings on the terrace with a laptop, a mobile phone, and her Martinis. She had papers which we surmised were received faxes. After lunch a taxi whisked her away to somewhere. On the Friday we had chosen to relax and unwind at the hotel. 'Sophisticated Lady' occupied her usual table on the piazza, but there were no Martinis! The bar, though open, was without the 'Manager'. The lady kept looking at the bar and around the hotel precinct. She did a bit more paperwork, got up and walked to the bar, again looking anxiously around for the missing, 'Drinks Dispenser'. Twenty minutes elapsed and Madam Barmaid's laugh was heard on the lower patio. The waiter had noted the lady's annoyance and reverted to his auto-pilot mode. He went behind the bar, prepared the drink for the lady and delivered it to her. She immediately ordered a second one. The waiter returned to the bar, recorded the transaction and prepared another Martini. As he was about to deliver it, he was accosted with a verbal tirade from, 'Madam Bar Manager.' He ignored her and delivered the Martini, then returned to his seat and newspaper. The bar reverberated to a remonstrance by the 'wildcat' who objected to him invading 'her' bar.

The owner, a rather portly Italian became aware of the disturbance. He came and took the wildcat's side, not wishing to be made aware of the 'Sophisticated Lady's' annoyance. The waiter, having retreated to his newspaper without retaliation, was sought by the owner who was obviously in reprimanding mode.

'Sophisticated Lady', hearing the raised voices, walked over to the Manager and intervened. She announced that she was doing research for Thompson Travel of England, Jetsave of New York and a Video Production Group making travel programs for the likes of the BBC. She said that the waiter was the only good thing about this crummy hotel and, if the waiter was given any aggro or troubled in any way, because he had given her some service when there was none other forthcoming, she would write a disparaging report about this hotel. She was sure that he, the Manager, would find his British clientele in decline. Then demanding to be brought another 'free' Martini she returned to her papers and all aggravation ceased. Soon the piazza fell into its normal morning somnolence.

At dinner that night she confided in us that she had, that afternoon, taken her taxi to one of the grandest hotels in all Europe, the Villa D'Este in Cernobbio near Como. She described the rooms as almost like museum galleries and said that the hotel boasts a floating swimming pool. She told us to go and have a walk round the hotel as it was well worth a visit. She said that through her executive-type occupation she was well acquainted with the manager and major-domo of this, as she described it, most illustrious hotel. She had told them about the gem of an English waiter who was being wasted at the Hotel Balionie and would most likely be happy to work in their establishment at any rank. Being acquainted with her knowledge, expertise and judgment in such matters she had convinced them that they should give him a try. And that this meal might be our last meal with him serving us.

She said she was still seething from the morning fracas, which we must have observed. She was checking out the following morning and chuckled as she showed us the note she was leaving with her bill.

It read "I used the extensive information in your brochure before I visited Lake Como district. I must say that your write-up on your hotel had me searching out for the Hotel Balionie until I found it, and then wished that I had not. I had been told that I could not get a bad meal in Italy. Your Restaurant proved that theory to be erroneous. Perhaps things have changed since you produced your brochure. The service was so inadequate that I had to wait 30 minutes for a drink in an empty lounge. You, the owner, didn't know or care what was going on. Yours is not a hotel to which I would recommend anyone. My experience will be related on our travel TV programmes."

Caroline d'Aulaire

Five Seasons Travel.

On our last day we did go down to the Villa D'Este in Cernobbio. It was way above our finances, but we did have afternoon tea and nobody seemed to mind us having a tour around. Who do you think served us with our very expensive afternoon tea? Our waiter. He had been embarrassed to find that our lady had thought so highly of him. He was however pleased that his new employer believed her. He reasoned that a manager of a hotel of this standard would be able to discern at a glance whether one had the expertise and experience of hotel service that is required to uphold the standards of the Villa D'Este. He added that the clientele was the sort that expected his class of service. His new, sumptuous, environment was especially suited to his interests and abilities. In the very short time he had found such favour with the management that he was able to talk them into employing the candyfloss-haired student. She was to start there the next day, but not serving on tables. He had been thinking of her studies and said that she would find a plethora of artefacts within the hotel which will give her a wealth of opportunity for study. It would have the added bonus that she could do it at her leisure and sometimes on the Company's time. He said with a smile, there was, however, a condition that she covered her head or otherwise hid it for the rest of this season. If offered work next season she must, before returning, pay a visit to a coiffeur who did not have the same sense of humour as her present stylist.

THE BUDDING BUCCANEER

When I was young I thought I would, like to be a sailor.
I'd sail across the seven seas, and maybe be a whaler.
I'd heard that there was lots of fun, just messing about in boats.
I also thought it might be fun, rubbing shoulders with cut-throats.

I practised how to tie the knots, I had to know the ropes.
Everything was magnified, peering through telescopes
I learned tintinnabulation, to understand eight bells.
But I was on the wrong tack, it is time that that bell tells

Navigation was such a headache, with many a 'bum' steer.
Without a bit of land in sight, it could have cost me dear.
Starboard and port were right and left, a poop is on the stern.
I couldn't find the place to poop, most embarrassing to learn.

I thought I'd see some dolphins, leaping, but none came near.
I had segs upon my eyeballs, and it was, in a leap year.
I also learnt that Mal de mer, is French for sea-sickness.
It's a malady that makes one doubt one's own seaworthiness.

In truth I learnt to hate the sea, horizons I abhor.
Never still, they go up and down, just like a child's see saw.
I don't care if I end up with egg upon my face.
I'll never make a buccaneer, terra firma is my place.

*   *   *

ANNE OREXIA

There was a silly girl one day,
Who would not eat her dinner.
She would not eat it any day,
And she got so much thinner.
Two fingers would go round her waist,
She was emaciating.
She said that she had lost her taste,
And fell right through a grating.

RETREATING FROM KHARTOUM

Back in February 1884, we were all in good spirits. We took a month to travel from Berber to Khartoum and arrived with General Gordon, as we thought, to help the Egyptian forces to defend Khartoum against the mad Mahdi. The General cheered us when he told us that his orders were to supervise the evacuation of the Egyptian forces and then we were to withdraw.

Not a month had passed before the Mahdi had besieged the city. Despite the siege, we had held out and more than a thousand women and children, together with sick and wounded, had been successfully sent down the river.

We had repulsed many attacks on the garrison, but, despite Government orders to evacuate Khartoum, it became evident that General Gordon was disregarding his orders, or they had been changed. In late October word had reached us that General Joseph Wolseley was on his way with a force of British soldiers from Egypt. We learned later that General Gordon had determined to hold Khartoum and felt that we could hold out until we were relieved. All the Egyptian troops had been given their orders and were eager to be on their 2000mile journey down the Nile and back to Cairo.

I was, as things turned out, very fortunate to be wounded in the arm during a skirmish between some Dervish scouts and my patrol. I then became a, 'Walking Wounded' and was to embark on one of three barges which would take fellow wounded and myself on the long journey to Cairo where we would be treated in a proper hospital. Despite our wounds, we were all excited.

There were fifty-six wounded on my barge, twenty-two of which were seriously so. I was detailed to help a nurse in any task that she instructed, if I had the strength so to do. The doctor who also acted as a surgeon was to oversee all medical needs on all three barges during the trip. The Egyptian soldiers were an escort to protect us on the way.

Our nurse, Agnes, busied herself arranging where each, on his stretcher should be placed. She was giving much comfort to our less fortunate comrades, while five able-bodied Egyptian chaps were busy loading the barge with victuals for the first leg to Dongola. They stayed aboard as guards on the trip. I waited on our nurse's every word and followed her like a puppy. "Fetch a blanket, fetch water, fetch more bandages." Three days of sailing had passed. Nurse Agnes had organised us, less wounded, by giving us tasks and duties. She had more organising ability than our Sergeant Major. We had morning prayers and she had us singing and swapping stories in the evenings when the barges were tied up. 'Soldiers of the Queen,' was our favourite and we sang it every night. We sang it so many times that the Egyptians copied and used it to try out their English.

There are places on the River Nile where there are cataracts. Some where the water is fast flowing; others where there is a maze of small rocky islands. At these points the boat felt as if it were on the high seas and as we passed through these, that was where Nurse Agnes was at her most attentive.

Two weeks passed and one night Nurse took me aside and said, "We must thank the Lord for those of our party who are getting well, but Private Higgins may not survive to reach Cairo." Higgins in fact died two days later. After that she talked a lot to me about her hopes for our worst-off.

The night before reaching Dongola I was writing my standard letter to my Mary, hoping that it would catch some post leaving as we were arriving. Nurse Agnes saw me and asked, "Writing home corporal?"

"Not really miss," I said, "You see, I cannot write properly. Sergeant taught me to write, 'I am well and I love you.' That has been on four letters that I have sent, but I have been able to write my name for a long time."

She was surprised and in her desire to help, asked, "Would you like me to write a letter for you?"

Of course, I was so pleased. She helped me choose all sorts of words that I would not have written, even if I known them or had been able to write for myself.

Dipping into the ink she asked, "What is her name, your wife?"

"Mary," I said, "but I have a daughter Charlotte and they cannot read."

"Then they will need to get someone to read it for them. That won't be very difficult."

She pulled the paper nearer to her and began to speak as she wrote, "Dear Mary, no we will write, My dearest Mary and Charlotte, that sounds better don't you think?"

How could I disagree? It sounded wonderful.

She continued, "I hope this letter finds you and Charlotte well. I love you both and long for the day when I can see you both again."

"I am well enough, but have a wound to my arm. It is not so much, as I am called a Walking Wounded. We are at present on a boat going down the river Nile to Cairo. 'Stop me if there is anything you want me to say.'" She continued to write, "With lots of brave men who are hurt much worse than I. When we get to Cairo we will all be looked after in a fine hospital."

I asked her to say that I was helping her and that she is helping me to write the letter and that we had been with General Gordon and that it will soon be over and us back to home.

She said she would, but asked, "First, have you any other family?"

I said "My widowed mother lives with Mary and Charlotte and me when I was at home. She has done so since my father died."

"Then, we will say, 'Give my love to mother,' shall we?"

I agreed saying, "What a wonderful thought. Mother will be so pleased to hear that."

"Yes," she said, "Just let her know that you are thinking about her also."

"And, how about, 'give Charlotte a kiss for me' and 'how I would like to give you one for yourself?'" she suggested.

She wrote about General Gordon, and that we would soon be home and at the end she finished with. 'Do not worry about me, my arm is getting better every day and God Bless you. Your loving husband John.'

Then she insisted "Now you must write your usual words, 'I am well and I love you.' That bit will be better if you write it."

I did as she suggested and after I had put my name at the end, she gave it to me as if to let me read it. But I could only stare or cast my eyes over it, such beautiful curvy writing. She could see that I was very pleased. Then she remembered that I was not able to read.

She asked, "Would you like me to copy it, and when we have some spare time I will teach you to read, you can practice reading with your own letter?"

I thought what luck this was, to be on this barge with her, so kind and so helpful and her promising to teach me to read.

Next day we arrived at Dongola where we found General Wolsely, Commander of all British forces in Egypt. He was personally taking his expedition up the Nile to help General Gordon. My letter went off to Cairo and then to England along with many of General Wolsely's dispatches and most likely some of General Gordon's.

After taking on supplies, we continued down to Luxor. Ten days passed as we slowly moved down the Nile. We passed some magnificent statues carved out of the rock at a place called Abu Simbel. We arrived at Luxor and stayed two days to take on more victuals. There were great Egyptian temples there which they said were over three thousand years old. It took another thirteen days to reach Cairo. Each evening of all these days Nurse Agnes would give me lessons and in the daytime, because there was very little paper to be had, I would practice writing with chalk on the deck. Above all, the great care that Nurse Agnes gave to the really wounded ensured that no more died and we all reached Cairo alive.

14 years have now passed, my wound healed with a slight disability to my arm. I am now with my Mary and I have given the kiss mentioned in the letter and many other kisses to her and Charlotte in person. Back in 1885, Khartoum, instead of being 'relieved,' had fallen. General Wolsely had some success by winning two victories with his advancing forces, such that the Mahdi was on the verge of raising the siege; but General Wolsely was delayed in reaching Khartoum. The Mahdi had seized his chance when the Nile waters fell sufficiently to expose a gap in the ramparts. The garrison was overrun and all were butchered.

General Gordon fell with them, having been stuck with the swords and spears of many Mahdi warriors, who no doubt attracted much acclaim in their ranks for being one of those who actually did the deed. A detachment of General Wolsely's forces under Charles Beresford, now Lord Beresford, arrived at the city on January the

28th just two days too late to find that General Gordon's head had been severed and presented to the Mahdi.

It is now 1898. Today I read in the newspaper 'Morning Post' that Major General Kitchener is, after all this time, on his way to retake Khartoum. He has upwards of 40,000 men and will most certainly prevail.

Yes, I am now able to read and write very well. I am gainfully employed on a regular basis running errands and copying for men of the judiciary, like a securely employed Mr Micawber.

Oh! The letter, I have it here in my pocket. I have read it a thousand times and, as I have said, I used it to practise reading before I had newspapers. I sometimes pretended that I had received my letter from Mary. They are such lovely words. I copied them many times. I was very fortunate to be on that barge with Nurse Agnes whose kindness in writing that letter has helped and taught me to read and learn lots of new words. Some fellows brought back souvenirs of Africa and others left bits of themselves there as commemoratives. But I have, as my souvenir, a great piece of literature, equal to any of Mr Dickens' writings. It is my letter to Mary.

* * *

CLEAN YOU'RE TEETH

Harry was a boy to scorn,
He would not clean his teeth.
The cracks were full of pop corn,
And little bits of meat.

He had a brand new toothbrush,
And tubes of minty paste.
His mouth was chock-a block with mush,
And what an awful taste.

In time his teeth went sooty black,
And all of them fell out.
He'll never ever get them back,
He wishes he'd washed out.

Wrrrr! it's cold in here tonight. Good job we all have fur coats. I'm glad I am not one of those over there in the window; they complain that it is very cold there. They stare out at the shutters all night. But there's some compensation that during the day they get lots of attention from passers by. We on the shelves, who are not so well admired, sometimes get the unwanted attention of sticky fingers, but if you are in the window you are out of the reach of the fingers belonging to children who want to look with their fingers and not necessarily their eyes. Some of their parents are just as bad. As well as using their fingers they can't read the 'No Smoking' sign. They come in with cigarettes dangling from their mouths. Puffing their smoke over us, they drop their ash everywhere and make us smell of tobacco.

Ah! Here she comes, fumble with the keys, unlock the door; dash to turn off the burglar alarm. Come on; put the heating on before you roll up the shutters. Daylight, that's much better!

Really I am a very lonely Teddy Bear. Sitting here for months waiting for somebody to buy me and take me to their home. I have never been in a home. Oh! Yes! I know all about homes. Some of the bears in this shop have been in many homes. They have told me stories of children who loved them; and loved them; but the children grew up, stopped loving them and had forgotten all about them. They often ask the question, "Where does love go when it dies?"

See that fellow over there, with his long legs hanging over the shelf and the button in his ear? He's German. He is from the family Steiff, or so he says. The others, for instance that lady bear over there on the counter, that one, they call her Winnie the Pooh, and she says that Steiff is worth a bob or two. She is from the Chad Valley.

See that chap, the one on that top shelf? He gets called Sooty, says he is Winnie's cousin. The bear over there on that other top shelf by the window, with a shelf all to himself, he is 50 years old. They call him 'Toffee,' and he claims to have been a BBC celebrity in a programme called, 'Listening with Mother.' He must be that old because none of the folk that come into this shop have ever heard of him. Fancies himself he does, in that knitted red hat and scarf. Oh yes! They all have tales to tell. Though I sometimes don't know what they are talking about. Take Stieff for instance, he says he has mohair, but it is more-like he has no hair, because he is nearly bald.

I have been sitting here for six months. Hardly anybody ever looks at me, except once a child, holding a chocolate iced cream around with the cream all about his mouth tried to pick me up with his sticky fingers. Madam, Her who runs this shop, quickly came to my rescue.

I wish there was a kind boy or girl to take me to a nice home, a home like the ones that Stieff and Winnie talk about. Do you know anyone who would like to have me? I would give them lots of bear hugs and love them to bits.

That smart fellow over there with the chequered pants and scarf has books written about him. See that pile of them on the stand by him? Well! I can 'Bearly' read, but the books say, 'Rupert' on them. His friend sitting beside him with the silly hat, those books on the stand near him, say, 'Paddington'. He is a real foreigner from a place they call South America.

See that one there with the bandage on his head, they call him Pudsey. He is a friend of a man named Terry Wogan. He has had that bandage on all the time that I have been here. It is about time his head got better. Wouldn't you think Mr Wogan would take him to the hospital?

I do hope I will soon be taken to a home where the children try hard to learn to read. Then they can teach me to read. We could go on picnics together. I understand that bears are famous for their picnics. Stieff told me that he went on one in 'Bearkshier' and he had honey. He also says that he has a sister named 'Beartha', she lives in 'Bearn,' somewhere in a place called Switzerland.

See the other stand by the books? They are 'Bearthday' cards that you can send to bears. I would like to get a 'Bearthday' card on my 'Bearthday.' In that big book on the counter there are lots of letters from Bears that have gone from here to nice homes. They write to Madam the shop-owner telling her what a nice place they live in; what they are doing with the children in their new homes. She makes a big fuss about those letters and tells everyone about them. One lucky bear went on a long holiday by the seaside. I have never seen the sea side but from what Stieff tells me, I think that would be nice.

Just by the side of the window, can you see a chap with a bowler hat and umbrella? Lived with a stockbroker he did. Likes to think he is a stockbroker too. I don't know what a stockbroker is, but he claims that the one he lived with made a lot of money in a hedge fund when there was a 'Bear' market.

What did that man say to the little girl? I am sure he said, "Which one do you like Princess?" A princess no less, we have never had a princess in here before. It is a Princess! He has just said, "What do you think Princess."

"Would you like Mr Panda Princess?" Then again, "No Princess; that one is called Schuco, she is special for ladies. Inside her tummy she has a bottle of perfume, maybe when you are grown up Princess, you will like perfume."

She must be a Princess! With the hundreds of bears here from which she can choose, she is taking a long time to find one that she likes, though it is good that she is looking with her eyes and not her fingers.

"Oohh! I think she is pointing to me. She is, pointing to me." Madam is coming to get me. Now she is holding me for the Princess to see me. I can now get a good close look at her. She is very pretty, she has long golden hair. I wonder if all princesses have long golden hair? What did I hear the man say? I thought I heard him say, "Yes he looks a very nice bear; I think you should have that one. Shall we have that one?"

"Princess, don't take so long in answering. Princess, Say yes! Say yes! Please say yes." To be loved by a Princess, that would be really something. That will get the others jealous and that will be one in the buttoned ear for Steiff. Wow! I am getting a hug! (Not so tight Princess.)"

"Yes I like this one daddy," she says.

She is hugging me and he is buying me. I know he is buying me because I have just heard the till go ding.

"A Princess; A Princess; Wowee a Princess; I'm going to live with a Princess."

*   *   *

THE COUNTRY CODE

When I go to the country,
It often makes me bitter.
To hear the noise that people make,
And see the tons of litter.

Should you go to the countryside,
To work or rest or play.
Here's a list of do's and don'ts,
To help you on your way.

Walk by lakes and mountains,
Valleys, dale and dell.
On country roads you watch your back,
Your front and sides as well.

Keep to the paths and close all gates,
Never breach the fences.
It is the farmer's livelihood,
Don't give him more expenses.

Livestock, crops and machinery,
Must all be left alone.
Keep your dog on a very tight lead,
Better, leave it at home.

Streams supply our water needs,
Year after year after year.
Don't, go picking and poking,
Leave them clean and crystal clear.

Protect the wildlife, plants and trees,
Be careful with your fire.
Especially when there's been no rain,
It is then the grass is drier.

If you always keep this code,
It isn't hard, now is it?
We'll have everlasting pleasure,
Whenever we care to visit.

When Snozzle Durante sang, "I'll celebrate. I'm feeling great, I'm the guy who found the lost chord," he could not have been happier than I who was about to celebrate, because I was feeling great. I was the guy who had just sold the Concord. I had just sold one of my paintings for £60. It was a picture of the Concord flying low over my headland.

Of course Concord never would fly low over any headland but my seascape background made it saleable. I was going to relax, I wouldn't even think about the Turner Prize. Well really, I am always relaxed, here in my own Shangri-la, with the wonderful views and the fresh sea air. The sun was melting the rocks. I thought; take the rest of the day off from my painting, that's what I would do.

First, I would go and check my night lines. It being a lucky day, I thought there was sure to be a two-foot turbot on my line. I set off crunching along the beach, which was a crescent of large pebbles, with other crescents of graded stones, finishing with a wide crescent of finely graded soft yellow sand where it meets the sea. Over the sand and pebbles were braids of seaweed, placed in perfect arcs which traced the shades of sand and gravel as if they were all drawn by him above, with a giant compass and unlimited number of shades.

This day the tide had not receded enough to show the sand. As I approached my lines I could see that I had caught something. The gulls were screaming and wheeling over my line. My, hoped for, two foot turbot would not have been safe for long. In a quarter of an hour the tide would be near its lowest, just right for them to clean the line.

When tending my line I always have to fight off the gulls, they turn their screams and sometimes their beaks at me. Near to my lines, I keep a piece of rope with a link of chain attached. By whirling it about my head I keep the gulls at bay. Sometimes the waves grow fierce to help the gulls. Both then keep me at bay and I usually lose. That day I was determined to win. As I paddled out, whirling the rope above my head like a South American Bolas I could see two plaice. Two, pan-sized plaice. I was in luck. Quick, untie the line and gather in my spoils.

I retreated to a favourite rock where I sat to unhook the fish and popped them into my M&S. all purpose carrier bag along with two smaller fish, one of which would become bait. Finding that my line had lost some hooks, I practised my fisherman's knots, and re-baited the hooks.

Waiting for the tide to return was no great chore. It was already at its lowest. It would not be long before it was on its way back and it had probably already done its turning. If the line was laid too early the gulls would get the bait. Nothing could be done except wait. I watched the gannets and terns fall like dive bombers to catch their fish and contemplated their underwater exploits. While waiting, I broke the promise I had made to myself, I did think about the Turner Prize. What piece of conceptual art would be suitable and would be a winner? From my favourite vantage point on the rock, I could take in the wonderful view. I marvelled at the way providence had placed that hill there for someone to build a castle. If it had been two hundred yards to the left it would not have been balanced. I had a similar thought about that lighthouse on the promontory. Further out to sea and the lighthouse would be out of the picture. On my right, the bay was defined by a mile of towering cliffs two hundred feet high. A bit higher or longer and they might have been out of proportion. Truly it was a beautiful place to be. I drifted off again, thinking, "What do I do about the Turner prize?" What would Turner himself make of that scene? I have a Turner in my studio, on the inside of the door; I have wiped my brushes on it for years. Greens, yellows, browns, good autumn tints, all randomly mixed streaks. It could well be a copy of his, 'Fall of the Clyde.' Mine is related to New Hampshire, I call it, 'The Fall.' I often imagine my door erected in the Tate Modern. I would be making peremptory statements like, "It is not the artist's job to answer questions about his conceptual art."

I picked up a handful of sand and examined the grains. Got it! How about a handful of sand, some slipping through the fingers, I thought, call it Melagueta, 'Grains Of Paradise.' My bay could easily be the shore of a Paradise Island.

The sun, which had been melting the rocks all day, had sunk to touch the top of the cliff, casting its glow over the beach, turning all the pebbles and the lighthouse from white to gold. What a sight. The pebbles at the high water mark are well-worn, nearly spherical stones, about the size of ostrich eggs. If I could have taken to the Turner exhibition a square metre of those golden stones, just as they were, I would have had a winner. I would have numbered them of course so that they could have been transported and placed in their original configuration. It wouldn't do to have one misplaced.

I could see a ship far out to sea. Not, I thought, a 'Dirty British coaster', with a salt-caked smokestack' nor a Quinquereme. Ships today are less aesthetic; they do not have smoke drifting back for miles to the horizon. But a Quinquereme beached on my shore, would have been very acceptable. It was unlikely that the ship out there was British. It was more likely to have been flying a flag of convenience. It occurred to me that a flag placed over my privy would be a 'Flag of a Convenience.' How would the Turner judges have considered that? 'Raising the artist's colours,' no doubt?

They seem to have a penchant for items of art which pertain to bodily functions. But then I thought it likely that a privy would not be sufficiently nauseating.

Casting about for further inspiration I noticed some fox footprints and some Canidae calling cards. Now, I mused, if I could arrange for some dogs to strategically place their droppings on the approach to a school, such that the Mums had to negotiate their prams around the droppings. I could have called it 'The Academia Slalom Run.' I soon dispensed with that idea as its title would have been a bit too obvious and would have eclipsed the 'Conceptual' sense. I remembered that similar material from an "Elephas maximus" was used in 1999, the judges eulogized and said it had, 'Emotional intensity.' Actually it was a load of old elephant poo.

The sun had gone down behind the cliffs and the sky was on fire. I wondered whether I could take a slice of that and call it 'Combustion.' No, I convinced myself, it must have a conceptual element. How about, 'Lustre After.' I imagined a judges' comment, "Cerebral."

The tide had crept up. An impatient crab appeared from under a rock to make a dash, like a line dancer, to the water. Could I cut it in half, pickle it in formaldehyde and call it 'CR' or 'AB'? No again. Better to leave it to enjoy its life in my Paradise.

The tide had collected, and was pushing its band of bric-a-brac mingled with sea-weed up the shore. A piece of bleached driftwood was trying to grip the stones; it might have been floating in the sea for years. If it could get a grip on the stones it might spend years drying out before a mighty storm grabbed it back to the water. I thought I would help it, it would stay outside my cottage and it might give me inspiration.

The fire in the sky had been extinguished. The tide had well covered my bait and the gulls had lost interest. It was way past time for me to pick up my catch of two 'pan-sized plaice' and return along the beach to the lighthouse jetty. How would 'A Pan-Sized Plaice in a round house,' grab the judges?

From the jetty, more like a natural flat stone with a couple of iron mooring rings, I have to climb the sixty-seven steps to my keeper's cottage. There are no keepers as such nowadays. When there were keepers they were paid to be here. What a lovely job that must have been. To be paid for living here. The ships that now pass in the night do so with electronic tentacles, gone are the beams of candle-light. The array of horns that are now attached to the lighthouse would lead you to believe that it is the abode of a stereophonic maniac.

The beach was littered with nature's artefacts, mingled with pieces of flotsam, or was it jetsam? There was a broken pulley-block trying, like the driftwood, to make it ashore. I thought about its heritage and what an interesting story it could tell, maybe of a Force Ten Norwester; the Battle of Trafalgar; the sinking of the Titanic or perhaps the 'Wreck of the Hesperus'. It could have made its way here from the Inchcape Rock and have been blessed by the Abbot of Aberbrothok. I considered it of little use for conceptual art as it was obviously part of a pulley block. But, then I changed my mind. If I added a bit of seaweed and called it, 'Submission to High Tension?' Would that electrify the judges? They would surely identify with the sheer 'Mental, emotional, and nervous strain' I had just, in that minute, undergone to produce my masterpiece.

Climbing the steps laden with fish, driftwood and other items in my M&S holdall, the view was breathtaking. Each time I stopped to get my breath, there was another, different, breathtaking view, even though the 'Painter's' light was gone. On reaching my cottage I deposited my day's collection in the paddock with many previous collections of priceless pieces of natural art. My wife, philistine that she is, calls it the wood pile.

Although I had literally, enjoyed, but wasted a whole day just,

'Smelling the metaphoric roses,' my wife had been hard at work preparing a meal for us. I am very lucky.

Unfortunately I did not have any luck with the Turner prize. I entered two spherical stones mounted on a piece of driftwood, entitled 'Neptune's Boules.' I understand that one of the judges thought it had, 'No artistic merit' and another thought it was, 'Rubbish.' But I was unaware that any of the judges possessed such artistic or aesthetic discernment in any great measure.

The winner was, "My Bed." A bed, created by Tracy Emin in one of her seminal moments, had tickled their aesthetic sensitivities. It was, they said, "An aesthetic arrangement of a bed complete with dirty sheets, blood stained knickers, used condoms and other apparently carelessly, but charmingly, discarded refuse, putting it in my words, "The detritus of indiscriminate sexual activities." Even though it was a Turner Winner I wouldn't want it in Paradise with me.

* * *

FIDDLERS FREE

Since I was voted to be an MP, for a middle England constituency.
I'd never need to touch my pay; I could save the lot for a rainy day.
I took advice from all my peers, and settled all my bank arrears.
I claimed a mortgage I hadn't got, and dossed in with my auntie Dot.

One didn't need to be discreet, or record on a balance sheet.
Fictitious claims could stretch a mile; things I claimed would make you smile.
I once claimed for a steeple Jack, to go and point the chimney stack.
On a mortgaged house I do not own, but got an increase on the loan.

My voters are devoid of brain, to go and vote me back again.
To voters I will thank and drool and send my kids to a very posh school.
The new rules do somewhat constrain, but I am not one to complain,
I'll make my *hypocritic* oath and carry on just like a sloth.

I'll never ever defy the whips; I'll go on lots of jolly trips.
I never ever declare my gain on my accruals from legerdemain.
I'll barely mention my hardship and someday make it to lordship.
Oh! And I forgot to mention I am in line for a very fat pension.

Twenty five or so, years ago I was standing, no, dancing, on the Kop at Liverpool Football Ground. Perhaps I was even levitating. So too were my Granddad and Nana. Such was our excitement at our team being five-one up on aggregate and F. C. Zurich was losing the semi-final of the European Cup. At Zurich Liverpool had won 3-1. Now, on our home ground, Liverpool was winning 2-0. With ten minutes left to play we were in high spirits. Then, Goaaaaal! I am sure that Granddad's leap was higher than Olga Korbut's famous Olympic feat of 1972. It was now a 'Fivemality' we were another goal up. The team was going to Rome! The team had already won the League Championship and were hoping to be the first team to win three trophies in one season. The FA Cup Final was to follow on the following Saturday.

Granddad, seventy four years old, and Nana 72 were avid Liverpool supporters, each holding annual season tickets. These were purchased every year as the standing collective Christmas present from the family.

For the special occasions, such that this was, Granddad always wore a distinctive red and white tricorn hat, and homeward, on the 'Mersey Snail,' he was the centre of attention. Of course he was bubbling with good cheer and clairvoyance. At the final, Brussia Mönchen Gladbach would be *aniliated*.

All week he was scanning the Echo. This company and that company were offering package trips to Rome. He must go, but could we afford it? What would it cost?

The euphoria was abated and there were sad hearts on the Saturday when Man United stole the F. A. Cup which put an end to that year's dreams of trebles. It was now impossible to deter Granddad from his desire to take Nana to Rome, even though there was no hope that they could ever afford the expense.

Granddad was not a well man. Mum and Nana did not know whether he knew it or not, but he had trouble which could see him off in a month or maybe years. Looking back it was likely that he knew and hoped that he would die with it, but probably not of it.

Again family rallied round. But, what if his sickness struck him while he was away? Well what if? What better time would there be for him to pop his clogs, than just as Liverpool scored the winning goal at a match that won the European Cup. The decision was made: Family club up and get them there.

All was arranged and we were all at Liverpool Airport to see them off. There were thousands and thousands of supporters. A veritable sea of red and white engulfed the airport, but only a comparative few lucky ones boarded planes destined for Rome. Granddad and Nana were two excited and apprehensive supporters amongst those lucky few. He wore his special tricorn hat and Nana wore her red and white cardigan.

All the passengers on their plane were on the same package tour and soon developed an Esprit De Corps particular to the group. All their tickets were for the same section of the ground and all were to be fed and watered in the same hotel. Granddad's hat, as usual, attracted attention, as did they both due to their years. Bonhomie and bon mot abounded.

"*av a drink* on me *Ma*," said one, later to be known as Willy, as he offered Nana a can, '*bu done*' open it till '*yeh ger*' on the plane, the ground staff are all Tea-Total."

"*Ere 'ave my seat Ma.*"

"*Like yer at Pop!*" . . . and that was only in the departure lounge.

First hurdle on the plane, find their seats. They were lost.

"What number *ar yis pop.*"

"*Yer 'ere* in front of *uz.*" Willy said, after he had examined their tickets. "Sit down *an' fasten yer* belt ready for inspection by the 'Trolley Dolly'." He continued, "*done worry, Me an' my mate 'arry 'll,* look after *yus, wone we 'arry?*"

Harry, or 'arry,' was Willy's travelling companion. Both seemed to be seasoned travellers.

Nana dutifully sat in her seat and fumbled with her belt.

Willy still being attentive said, "This is the way *yer fasten yer* seat belt."

Harry equally helpful asked "'*Ave yer* never flown before?"

Nana confided that this was her first time on a plane.

Willy consoling said, "*A tol' yer, done* worry, *gerra* couple of brandies *down yer and yus wone be frightened of nothing*".

"*Ere Ma, ave this one on me*". Said Harry as he offered her a slug from a brandy bottle, but seeing that she declined to drink from the bottle he produced some plastic cups from an M&S carrier bag.

"*Eer av it in this cup* the 'Trolly Dolly' will think it is lemonade, they don't like you to bring your own booze on board."

He then turned his attention to Granddad, "*Eer pop you av one too.*" He then poured for Willy who was holding a cup.

The time went quickly while each told each their family history; where they always stand or sit in the ground; who had scored the best ever goal. The list was endless.

At the hotel, having checked-in, they made their way to their room. Willy was still playing chaperone and on entering the lift said, "Don't think much of the rooms in this Hotel this one is awful small."

Later having been fed and watered Nana and Granddad were in the hotel lounge.

Willy in high spirits saw them and asked, "*Yer not go in out on the town? Come wi' us.*"

Feeling that there was safety in numbers, they ventured out. The group found a bar where the decor had been arranged to attract the, 'Red Brigade' and settled in, bidding all comers a rowdy welcome as if they had known them from childhood.

Next morning Granddad and Nana were taken in hand again, "*Cum wi' us we'll show yous* the Glories of Rome. *Y've 'eard of one of the Glorias 'aven't yer*? She's in Excelsior, just down the road at the Vatican."

Everywhere was red and white and a stuck in the groove record was repeating "WE ARE THE CHAMPIONS! WE ARE THE CHAMPIONS!"

The Vatican steps were covered with Liverpool supporters. Harry, pointing to the sea of red said, "*Ay Willy, I bet yu'v* never seen that many *wiatin'* to go to mass. I wonder '*ow* do they sell the '*oly* water? It would be great to take a gallon '*ome.*"

Don't get lost Pop, '*ang* on to Willy's coat, *bu'* don't 'For God's sake,' touch the hem or miracles might happen, Gladbach might win."

The Trevi Fountain was amassing the entire output of the Italian mint. All offerings from the Red Army were accompanied by the same wish. Some Germans, still high on their win of the world cup three years before, were claiming that their contrary wishes would prevail.

They were asked, "How much have you thrown in?"

"Between us, fumfzehn Million, fifteen million Lira,"

"We can do better than that, can't we lads?" So they threw Willy in.

Willy was, at that time, clad only in his red shorts, which later gave him a red hue to his legs. He later became very proud of his red legs, although he claimed that he was from a 'Blue Stocking' family.

Food and drink were difficult to obtain. Cafés and bars were crowded. It was decided that one of them would fight his way to get a bulk order of Pizza even though the prices were a rip-off.

Well in advance of kick off, all gravitated to the stadium with sounds of, "WE ARE THE CHAMPIONS! WE ARE THE CHAMPIONS!" guiding the way as if by sonar.

Inside the ground, having been jostled into what seemed to be a good vantage point, everyone waited impatiently.

Some great excitement was generated when Emlyn Hughes and Kevin Keegan ventured out with Berti Vogts to inspect the pitch.

"Wharrer they *doin frattin' wi de enemy?"* asked Willy indignantly.

Time to start; both teams emerged to a roar that proved that the walls of the stadium were stronger that those of Jericho, and silence as the referee blew the starting whistle.

Now, "WE ARE THE CHAMPIONS," was punctuated with, "ooh!" and "Aahh!" and "We're *gonna* win the cup, *we're gonna win* the cup, ee-I-addio, we're *gonna* win the cup."

Of course the Germans were likewise cheering their team on with equal tumult, but a 'red favour' rendered one's ears impervious to the sound of such uttering.

Approaching half-time, a scuffle at the German end and the ball was back and forward like a fiddler's elbow. Suddenly Terry McDermott had it in the German net. The crowd erupted into whoops of delight, jumping and dancing, pushing, shoving and hugging. It was as if someone had kicked the hive of red bees.

These transports of delight were abruptly brought to an end when Simonsen scored for the Germans, the score was even. A state of paralysing dismay overtook the reds.

"Wir sind die Besten! Wir sind die Besten! Wir sind die Besten!" could be heard clearly. But only for a minute.

"WE ARE THE CHAMPIONS! WE ARE THE

CHAMPIONS!" was renewed with more vigour drowning out the Wir sind die Besten.

The second half started with many more "Oohs!" and "Aahs," lips were bitten, and near heart failures until, twenty minutes from time, there was an eruption, easily fifteen on the Richter Scale. Tommy Smith had scored. Then there was an exponential decrease in the cheering as fingers were crossed, lips were now bitten to shreds. Time went slowly, as the sound of, "You'll never walk alone," began to grow to a crescendo. Ten minutes to go, and the last time so many prayers were offered simultaneously from Rome the Pope had died.

Three minutes from time. Keegan was on the floor in the box. Berti Vogts had his hands up in supplication. The referee's hand was also up, in what could have been a Hitler salute and his whistle sounded like heavenly trumpets.

Silence. Phil Neal was approaching the penalty spot. The inter heavenly communication system must have surely blown a fuse

God would have turned off all reception from Rome; and the ball was in the back of the German net.

All over the world vulcanologists were indicating that the epicentre of this seismic happening was Rome.

"What's the matter Pop?"

"Why are you *sittin'* down? *Wharra yu* crying for?"

Nana was also crying. And they were not the only ones crying. Machismo was dead for a while.

"On *yer* feet Pop, Emlyn's *go' na* lift the cup."

There was more pushing and shoving and renewed euphoria which persisted throughout the lap of honour. Euphoria which persisted for the interminable time it took to get out of the stadium, grab some more food, return to the Hotel for their personal belongings and of course lots of 'scoops.' Euphoria as they helped to carry comrades who were now worse for wear, to await the bus to take them to the Airport.

Even at two o'clock in the morning a cacophony of, "WE ARE THE CHAMPIONS, WE ARE THE CHAMPIONS" could be heard from the departure lounge as the differing groups awaiting different planes competed with their shibboleth. Eventually some fell asleep on the floor until the loud speaker announced, "Will passengers for flight LIV1694 to Liverpool make their way to gate 5.

"That's *uz! Cum* on Pop, *cum* on Ma, wake up"

All awakened to renew the rejoicing with yet another raucous chorus of WE ARE THE CHAMPIONS," which persisted as they left the terminal and did the conga out to the plane. Some with jelly legs found it difficult to hang on to those in front of them as they stumbled up the stairs and on to the plane.

Unheeded on the plane was the voice saying, "Will passengers please be sure they take their allotted seat."

"Willy you are in the wrong seat." Granddad was now looking after Willy and was making him change seats.

"Good job you showed me how to fasten a seat belt," Granddad said as he made an effort to fasten Willy's belt.

"Leave it unfastened," said Willy, "the 'Trolley Dolly' will fasten it for me, she's *gorgis*."

Then came the voice of the Captain, "Good morning everyone, I trust you have had a pleasant stay in Rome."

To which there was a "Yeah!" and a chorus of, "WE ARE THE CHAMPIONS, WE ARE THE CHAMPIONS."

"In that case," said the Captain, "It looks as if we are all 'flying high,' I hope the success does not go to your head."

There was another, "WE ARE THE CHAMPIONS, WE ARE THE CHAMPIONS."

At the take off, the 'Trolley Dolly,' having checked the seat belts went to her station to demonstrate the safety procedure. Her arm, hands and waist movements could have been choreographed by Diaghilev himself. The voice over saying "Will drop from above;" "fasten behind your back," her hands were weaving like Salome's.

When she had finished there was a call of "Encore, more! more! more! Do it again."

Eventually, all, well nearly all, were asleep and all was quiet for hours. Later they were awakened by the 'Trolley Dolly' nudging those with unfastened seatbelts. An indication that they were, already, or soon to be, descending. And one last joker went about the cabin with a hat, collecting for the driver.

In the Arrivals Hall, at eight o'clock in the morning, amid "WE ARE THE CHAMPIONS, WE ARE THE CHAMPIONS!" there were long goodbyes to the now life-long friends who were vowing to see each other on the following Saturday.

Mum and I had been waiting for hours for the return of the victors. From the moment they extricated themselves from their new-found friends we were to hear about every highly charged minute of the thirty-seven hours. We were hearing about it for years and years and years. I think it rejuvenated my Granddad.

* * *

VALENTINES DAY IS HERE AGAIN

I'd rather you do the dishes,
Than send a valentine.
The sum of all my wishes,
You'd do them just one time.

I'd rather you do some painting,
Than buy a rose for me.
But I am tired of waiting,
In my scruffy scullery.

I'd rather you use the vacuum,
Than draw some bleeding hearts.
Or be a lawn mower mover,
Before the football starts.

I don't want frilly panties,
Through which anyone can see.
They were alright in my twenties,
But now I'm fifty-three.

I don't mind lots of kisses,
To show that you love me.
I'm happy to be your Mrs,
Without Valentine frippery.

"What are you doing now?"

"I'm making the bed."

"Well leave it. Leave it open, it will air the beds and be healthier." Shouts daddy.

"But it's so untidy."

"You're too fussy, who's going to see it? Only Father Christmas, and he is not coming here. Anyway we said we'd be on the road by ten o'clock and it's now ten past twelve. Leave it now."

Mum reluctantly left the untidy beds. As she descended the stairs, she called the two children to get into the car. The car was packed with personal baggage for four; Christmas presents, some secret, some well pored over, and some rather untidily parcelled. There was also food; a turkey and a Christmas cake, which Mum had baked and iced. Two Teddies were already strapped into the centre seat. There were also enough victuals for a three-week safari. But they were starting a four-hour journey.

The children made their way to the car while Mum collected coats, scarves and gloves which had been left in the hall. Dad was checking locks, water and heating for a house to be unoccupied for seven days. Mum fastened the children in their seat-belts saying, "Before we start, have you got your presents for Granny and Granddad?"

"Yes," enthused Greg, "and we have Daddy's as well."

Mum did not want to confuse the situation by asking, "Have you got mine?" So she proceeded to her seat and fastened her belt.

Dad locked the front door and, after removing his coat placed it on a bedding roll which was now between the children and suffocating the Teddies.

Halley, full of questions, wanted to know, "Daddy, are we going to camp at Granny's?"

"No," said Daddy, "you will have the same bunk as you had when we visited Granny for her birthday."

"Then why are these sleeping bags here?"

"You will need big bags for all the presents that Father Christmas will be bringing, and they are the biggest I can think of." and with that Daddy climbed in and fastened his belt.

Putting the key in the ignition he said to all, "Have you all brought everything you need? Where did we put that new 'Beetle' that we bought for Mummy?"

Greg, ten years short of being street-wise claimed, "We didn't buy a car for Mummy."

As the car moved out of the drive, Mummy spoke in a low, joking voice saying, "I'm disappointed that I'm not getting a car, and why have we brought bedding rolls?"

"You women wouldn't think of such things, while you wash kids and make beds, but the weather forecast is not good, that's why I have been pestering you to get going. If it gets cold they can get into the rolls."

All was quiet from the back for some thirty miles, except for Greg's question, "Are we stopping at the Little Chef Daddy?"

"I don't want to, but we will have to stop and buy some drinks or something there so that you can have a wee."

Small talk followed, about which drink would be preferable, and another forty or so miles passed by.

Mummy, remembering the forecast conversation, observed, "It doesn't look too good does it?"

"No it doesn't" Daddy said thoughtfully, "it said we could get snow on high ground; if you look over there where we are heading, it doesn't look-."

Mum cut in saying "Look at that car over there, it has snow on it, I wonder how far it has come with that?"

"Don't wonder any longer, there's some on our windscreen now."

Soon the windscreen was covered, visibility was getting difficult and the heater was directed from feet to the windscreen. It had some little effect.

Daddy, concentrating and now driving with difficulty, said, more to himself than his passengers, "I shouldn't stop on this motorway to clear the windscreen but I am going to have to." Then way ahead he could see some flashing amber lights. He thought, an accident, but as he approached it, he was relieved to find that it was a gritting lorry.

"I think," said Mummy "there's a Service Area near here."

There was an unconscious shake of the head as Daddy said, "I don't want to stop, I want to get as far as I can before dark."

"I know you want to get as far as you can but we could stop;

give you a rest and have some of our sandwiches."

"I suppose that's good thinking," said Daddy in agreement but it was thirty more miles on, that he had planned to have his rest.

It seemed as though lots of drivers were having a rest but a parking bay was found and Mummy handed out the food. Although it was snowing and there was much slush underfoot both children wanted to go to the loo. This allowed Daddy to have his rest but Mummy and the children returned like snowmen and with very wet feet. Mummy struggled to remove their wet top clothing and the sleeping bags were brought into service. A problem arose when it was found that sleeping bags do not readily lend themselves to seat belt encumbrance. Eventually all seemed safe and satisfactory, so Daddy reluctantly moved off.

They were in a long line of slow moving vehicles and it was now getting dark. Mummy rang Granny to tell her to expect their late arrival. The grit from the lorries was melting the snow on the road and, while the snow still fell on the windscreen, the salt in the slush which was thrown up by other vehicles helped the wipers to do their work. Daddy was again at full concentration, making 25 miles per hour. Nothing could be seen through the other windows except the glare of the risk-taking over-taker's headlights. Now and then the column stopped, and in this way they made slow progress in comparative silence with the 'stop, start, stop' for another hour and a half.

Daddy broke the silence and observed, "We will soon be coming to the Little Chef, if I manage to see it."

"Are you going to make another stop there," asked Mummy?

"We had better stop there, I need a break from driving and we are not on the motorway from there."

Mummy turned to the children, "Are you two awake? We will be at the Little Chef soon and we will buy hot drinks when we get there."

Mummy and Daddy, trying not to show their anxiety, peered through the dirty windows in the hope of seeing the Chef sign in time to turn off the motorway.

At last the big blue sign, partially covered with snow but still indicating, one mile to junction seventeen, came in view.

"This is it," said Daddy and, as the car turned and rose to the top of the exit ramp, they could see the Little Chef sign. Daddy pulled into the car park and noticed that the car park was full of cars and had not been gritted. As he stretched his arms and rubbed his eyes he said, "We have another fifty-something miles to go from here, I hope the roads have been treated."

Mummy was struggling with the children, putting on coats and shoes. This done, they ventured forth into the café which was packed with tired drivers. They had arrived within half an hour of closing time. Mummy suggested, "What say we have something substantial to eat, as we don't know how long we will be on the road?"

"I suppose we should. It will be nearly midnight before we get to Granny's, or we could be out all night," said Daddy, "and I will have a doze while you order me 'an early starter breakfast'."

After eating, mummy tucked the children into the sleeping bags again and Daddy scraped the new snow from the windows; cleaned the slush from the headlights and mirrors; climbed aboard, and fastened his belt saying, "Ten past ten."

There were fewer vehicles on these roads and the grit had not always done its work. Some parts were packed snow, but in villages the grit was doing its work. The wipers were again finding it difficult fighting with the snow, and Daddy had to stop twice to clear the screen.

After another hour and a half of very careful and tiring driving Daddy pulled in to buy petrol and scrape the windows again. He stayed on the forecourt for fifteen minutes having another rest.

The children were asleep and mummy woke from a little doze, "Where are we?" she asked.

"We made good time considering," said Daddy as he started the car again, "'I' was having a rest. We've about twenty-five miles to go. I reckon it will be after twelve when we get there."

Another ten or so miles on, at a part where the snow was unaffected by the grit, the car decided to waltz across the road. Daddy was frantically turning the wheel, trying hard to put into practice all the folk-lore he had heard about rectifying a skid. Fortunately there were no trees or street furniture to hinder the car in its cavorting, but it did mount the grass verge, skid backwards, and came to rest with wheels in a gully.

"What's happened?" said Mummy, with panic in her voice, and looking to the back seat where children were just wakening.

"Are you all-right?" enquired Daddy, meaning is everyone all right. The children said that they were but they really had no idea what had happened.

"I'm still in one piece," replied Mummy, "How are you?"

"It seems as though we have all been lucky," said Daddy as he loosened his belt and reached to put his arms around Mummy, "but I wonder whether the car is?"

They stayed hugging each other for some minutes before Daddy suggested he try starting the car. He took a torch from the glove box and went out into the snow to see if there was any damage. But there was none that he could see. The lights were still in working order but the back wheels were in a gully.

"We are not going to get it out of here without help," he whispered. "Make sure they are well wrapped up. It will get cold if we are here for any length of time with the engine turned off." Then he rummaged in the glove box for the AA details.

Just then the windows were lit as the headlight of another car pierced the snow covered windows. It had stopped and the driver called, "Are you al-right?"

Daddy went through the deep snow to talk to him. "Yes thanks. No blood spilt and we are just going to call the AA. I think we will be safe here until they come."

"I'll be on my way then." He waved to Daddy and started on his way shouting, "Good luck!"

Daddy climbed back into the warmth of the car and started to press numbers on the mobile as another brighter light appeared and the sound of 'Jingle Bells' could be heard. The vehicle stopped and after a minute or two, a hand started to wipe the snow from the windows as the owner of the hand peered into the car. "Anybody hurt" said a voice from outside as the car door opened and an elf peered in.

"No-one hurt, no blood spilt," Daddy said again. The music could still be heard outside.

Another elf appeared by the open door as the first elf said, "There are two children in here."

Then the hand which had been cleaning the windows opened the rear door where the children sat wrapped in the bed rolls. "HO! HO! HO!" said the man, who was dressed in red and had a white beard which now was gathering snow. "Are you well little ones?"

The children could not believe their eyes. Here was Father Christmas himself and he had stopped to see if he could help. Through the now-clear windows they could clearly see his sleigh on the back of a brightly-lit lorry, and there were reindeer too.

Seeing their surprised eyes he anticipated any questions, "I too needed some help in this snow. This kind driver has given us a lift on his wagon, reindeer and all! They are a bit tired, Ho Ho Ho!"

Daddy was now outside and talking to the six elves and the driver. The driver said, "We will soon get you out of here, I always have tackle for emergencies in case I get into trouble."

One of the elves brought a long rope and Father Christmas himself said, "Here give me the end and I will tie it to your car."

Father Christmas went on his knees and fastened the rope while an elf tied the other end to the lorry. "Come on Daddy get in and steer," instructed Father Christmas as he and the elves prepared to lift the back of the car out of the gully.

"Pull away!" he shouted above the sound of Jingle Bells, and the lorry started to move forward. "Now you elves, heave!" The back of the car came up out of the gully and moved forward on its front wheels. It was soon back on the road and the rope was loosed from the car. It was so exciting.

"Is it still a runner?" asked one of the elves. "Try it, and we will follow until you say it is OK."

Off went Daddy. Father Christmas climbed back onto his sleigh and the lorry followed Daddy.

They soon came to a village where Daddy stopped and went back to talk to Father Christmas. The children, straining in their belts to see through the back window, saw Daddy have a long talk and hand-shaking with the elves and Father Christmas. Then Daddy came back and set off again. He said to Mummy, "They will be following us to within five miles of Granny's where they are getting food for the reindeer." All the way they could hear "Jingle Bells, Jingle Bells."

Granny and Granddad were ever so glad to see them arrive. They had been out of their minds with worry,

The children excitedly exclaimed, "Do you know what happened to us on the way Granny"

"No I have been so worried," she said as she hugged them. "Granny," said Greg, "You won't ever believe it, but the car skidded and went into a ditch, and Father Christmas came along with his elves and his sleigh and his reindeers. They were getting a ride on a lorry because the reindeers were tired and they were going to get food for the reindeers. Father Christmas and his elves put ropes on our car and pulled it out of the ditch."

"Yes it was really, really Father Christmas, I saw him," added Halley.

Granddad joined in, "And all the time we have been worrying about you, you have been hob-nobbing with Father Christmas?"

"Yes," said the excited Greg, "and Daddy gave the elf some money."

"Why did you do that?" asked Halley.

"Oh, er," Daddy stammered, "It was really for the driver because he helped too."

*   *   *

A REGULAR ROYAL QUEEN

She hasn't got a proper job not one like yours or mine,
She's not a shop assistant nor on the assembly line.
What she really does I'm afraid I cannot tell,
But when she does, whatever it is, she does it very well.
I'm told she has great insight and can, if she thinks fit,
Dismiss her prime ministers who often have dim wit.
She can say stand up, while she sits down,
Especially, when she wears her crown.
She's had a lots of experience, more than sixty years,
Precludes anyone from claiming that she's wet behind her ears.
Talks with foreign dignitaries and keeps the common touch.
But at a social gathering she never, ever goes Dutch,
To hear sycophant's orations may get right up your nose,
They are hopeful of a gong or two, but make me bellicose.
But I suppose like all of us, she has her hopes and fears,
And now and then, like all of us, she's capable of tears.
With sixteen Regnal titles and Colonels thirty-four,
Defender of the faith and mother, could you ask for any more?
I don't think there's anywhere that she has never been,
But whether for or against her, let's shout, 'GOD SAVE THE QUEEN.'

It was Sunday morning; Granddad had the newspaper spread over the dining table. Gloria, an Italian paying guest, with half specs on the end of her nose, was sitting in an armchair reading another newspaper. Granddaughter Chloe and her mum Betty had arrived for the ritual Sunday dinner. Granny and Mum were bonding in the kitchen whilst preparing the food. Chloe was drawn, as usual, towards Granddad and Gloria.

Granddad's paper displayed a one-fifty-point headline 'CINEMA OWNER TO CHALLENGE SPIDERMAN'

Now Chloe liked the Spiderman stories in her comic papers, and was prompted to ask, "What is that story about Spider Man? Anyone who challenges Spiderman will surely lose."

"Well," said Granddad, "It is a long, complicated and serious story. You can see there is a whole page of it, but I'll try to shorten it. It is about a plague of spiders in a Cornish village."

Gloria pricked up her ears and began to listen.

"Ur," said Chloe, "A plague of spiders, I wouldn't be afraid of one or two, but a plague? That sounds terrible! But Spiderman would not be bothered, would he?"

Granddad continued, "Well that's what it is about, it seems as though this village is plagued with spiders, they are everywhere! The inhabitants have left or been evacuated. The town council have brought in a famous arachnologist with more letters after his name than the post office handle at Christmas. He claims that the endemic centre of the infestation is in the privately owned village cinema."

Chloe interrupted to ask, "What kind of spiders are they? Are they tarantulas?"

Granddad, adjusted his glasses and searched the columns saying, "It's here somewhere, oh yes, it says, 'They are called 'Ciniflo Fenestralis', they commonly live in sheds and outhouses. They are the species that makes the large polygon shaped webs in the windows.' "I suppose that figures," Granddad mused, "because leaded light windows like church windows are fenestrations," and, he continued, "this spider specialist, the newspapers dub him 'The Spiderman,' is all set to exterminate the spiders, but the cinema owner, a Scotsman, named Robert Bruce is objecting strongly and has barricaded himself into the cinema regardless of the spiders. Of course the villagers are up in arms at this. He does not care what qualifications an egg-head spiderologist has, he is not going to let him into his cinema."

Gloria asked, "Does he not want to be rid of the spiders?"

"It seems not," said Granddad and he continued the story, "The police, dressed in all sorts of space-man gear, have tried to remonstrate with the owner of the cinema, but he is adamant that he will not allow any scientist or Spiderman into his cinema to do the work. He, the owner, claims to be a descendant of the great 'Robert the Bruce.'

He said to the police, 'Wa *dees this egg heed, ken aboot speiders, shae he dinna ken the words o' auld Walter Scott's 'bonnie lass o' Perth', 'HE WAD BE AS LAITH. TAE WANTONLY DAUD AN KILL A PUIR WEE SPEIDER, AS IF HE WIS A CLANSMAN O' OOR AIN KING RAB, WI' A GUID MINDFU MEMORY.' FUR I AM WAN O' THEM CLAN. No kin of King Robert would ever daud a spider.*"

Grandad gave the newspapers interpretation of this as; 'What does this egg-head know about spiders? He does not know the lines of Sir Walter Scott's poem, 'The Fair Maid of Perth,' which go, 'He would be as loth. In wantonness.' Translated, 'He would be as unwilling to deliberately kill a poor spider, as if it were a kinsman of King Robert.' and he, the cinema owner, is of that kin. No kin of Great King Robert would ever harm a spider.'

"And that," said Granddad, "is where it is up to, the police cannot get in and Mr Bruce is not coming out,"

Enthralled, Chloe asked, "Who was Robert the Bruce?"

Granddad told the 'true' story of King Robert, having lost seven battles with the English King Edward; he watched a spider make seven failed attempts to link two points in the cave where he was hiding. On the eighth attempt the spider was successful. Robert thought he would have an eighth try, and he was successful. Have you not heard the saying, 'If at first you don't succeed, try, try and try again?'

Gloria, being Italian, and, despite her years, had never heard of King Robert, was equally spellbound, but asked, "How does the Spiderman plan to exterminate the spiders?"

"Well now," said Granddad, "it does say in here how he

intends to do it. But you can also see it on his 'web site', 'Spiderman. com.' After he has caught a good proportion of the spiders, many of the remainder are killed with insecticide. The caught ones are made impotent. It seems as though he and his helpers pull off their front legs. This, they say, alters their genetic make-up so that they are not able to lay fertile eggs. Eventually, not being able to reproduce successfully, they all die."

Chloe was beaten to the obvious bewildering question by Gloria, "You mean it will be done by the pulling off of their legs?"

"Yes," said Granddad, "just like I'm pulling yours."

* * *

ODE TO THE LADIES OF THE BARNSTON WI

To sooth the nerves from time to time,
A cup of tea can be sublime.
Darjeeling, Chinese or Siam,
It's better than Diazepam.

Some like their tea made in a cup,
But that's not how I like to sup.
I like mine poured out from a pot,
It keeps the next cup nice and hot.

It's nice to have a cup of rosy,
Taken from, a pot that's cosy.
A cosy made by a crafty hand,
With stitches under and overhand.

I, have such an appurtenance,
A cosy with great provenance.
You doubt how it came to such as I?
It came from the Barnston WI.

THE LONDON MARATHON

Thousands of people in the London sun,
Pleased to be running in the Marathon.
Pushing and jostling with smiling face,
Hoping to be first in this famous race.

Everyone with an altruistic bent,
Not running for self aggrandizement.
Though it's not evident at the first glance,
Charities are the appurtenance.

A Buddhist, Muslim and a Kosher Jew,
A Christian, a Sikh and a Hindu too.
All jogging along in an ethnic mix,
All with a differing double helix.

Great camaraderie, tempers intact,
Not governed by a Race Relations Act.
No tension shows over race or creed,
Not a care about any colour or breed.

Half way round and the going gets tough,
Some wish to quit, but they've not done enough.
All strain every muscle, nerve and sinew,
Forcing their bodies and minds to continue.

A group of front runners get a great cheer,
Signs that the finish is getting quite near.
It matters not who's first past the line,
So long as contestants have a good time.

The last stragglers come, worn out and tired,
All proud of the sponsor's money acquired.
What a world it would be if all of the nations,
Could espouse such blissful race relations.

We had been married only two-and-a-half years when my pregnant wife was diagnosed as having contacted a life-threatening virus. The doctors did all that they could. Unfortunately as some drugs were out of the question unless the pregnancy was terminated, she chose to terminate. The termination also had problems and she died a week later.

That was some five years ago. I ceased to be interested in the opposite sex and became a workaholic. Diligence at work had its compensations. I have climbed the ladder of promotion nearly to the top. It was as if the ladder of success was, in my case, lying flat on the floor. The dice seemed always to fall right for me and I made fast progress along the ladder. Regularly I moved up to a bigger and better office.

During this time some well-meaning friends tried to get me paired off, but all offerings seemed to lack the spark that would arouse any passion to get me interested. However, it was like waiting for a bus. You wait and wait and then two come along at once. Life suddenly became very complicated, juxtaposing two very, very desirable ladies and trying to keep them both regularly entertained. I was juggling evenings and sometimes days. Eventually I was backed into a corner and I had to extricate myself from one, but which one?

It all started with perfume. My PA. was about to be married, and as well as a wedding present, I felt that I owed her something personal for her services to the company. I knew that she sometimes, only on special occasions, had a very pleasing redolence. I had concluded that she had a special occasion perfume. Furtively I enquired of other staff what might be the name of this fragrance.

The answer soon came back 'La Nuit de Paco Rabanne' 1/2oz £118, very, very, chic. I suggested to the staff that I would supplement their generous collection and we buy some of this Paco as an extra to her wedding present. It would be an extra on the bonus she deserved.

I found this not so easy. Searching 'The Net,' directed me to Harrods and a special order was made from 'The House of Paco Rabanne'. I was able to take my place at the wedding as a guest armed with the two gifts.

During the reception, before the package was ever opened, all ladies present, seemed to be aware of the highly specialised gift. The bride, who knew nothing about it was prevailed upon to open it at the breakfast table. She was delighted. It of course would not have been on her wedding list. She recounted that ten or so years ago she had won a very small quantity of this precious liquid, but for this special occasion of her wedding she had now used all of her original supply.

It so happened that the Queen Bee of, 'Nouvelle *Cuisine*,' a firm of outside catering specialists, was in command of the victuals. I must say that her presence was to me, something special and I kept hoping that she would come around to me, over and over again, with her gourmet offerings. How could I engage her in conversation? Then she identified me as the perfume specialist and she opened the conversation. It had been five years, and here it was. I remember that my granddad had said, "You will know it when the right one comes along." It seemed that he was right.

She did not have a function arranged for the next day and things moved on apace.

A fortnight later I was awaiting my Queen Bee in the lounge of the Crown Plaza Restaurant when she rang to say that she must call the evening off. She sounded very disappointed, so was I. Just at that moment I got a whiff of the one perfume with which I am familiar. I could not mistake it, I thought it was telepathy but it was not. It was certainly 'La Nuit de Paco Rabanne'

Turning to see whose, I instinctively sniffed. Behind me was a creature such as you would find on the cover of Vogue, and she had seen me sniff.

Trying to cover my embarrassment I blurted out, "La Nuit de Paco" Her jaw dropped as I continued "Rabanne."

She recovered and said, "You are a connoisseur of perfumes?"

I turned my chair to face her and it happened again. Something, her face, her hair, her posture, I don't know but something in me said, "She is different." She said that she had actually stolen a sample of 'La Nuit' when at a perfumery course and that she was a perfumes salesgirl, named Gayle. Never had she sold any of this most expensive perfume, nor even seen any, except on the perfumery course. If a customer wanted some, it would have to be specially ordered from The House of Paco Rabanne. So how could I single it out? We talked and talked. After a while she ventured to say that she thought she had been 'stood up'. I lied that I had suffered a similar fate, suggesting that, despite our disappointments there was no reason to waste the evening and that we should go into the restaurant together.

She countered with, "Only if we go Dutch." I agreed to her request, but determined that I would eventually pay, as sales girls do not usually pay for dinners in the Crown Plaza. She had surely expected her date to foot the bill. Or he had chickened out.

Over dinner, I explained how I had gained my specialist knowledge of perfumes, well one particular perfume, but I did not mention the Queen Bee.

While we were talking I thought, 'She is fantastic.' It had happened again. Granddad had told me that with some people it could strike twice. He was right again.

I saw her to her home and arranged to see her again, and again, and again. This was not too difficult as my Queen Bee was not available every night. But I remember when she first kissed me. Conversely it turned me *into* a toad. From then on I was cheating on one or both of them. I remembered another of Granddad's sayings. "It is better to kiss a miss than to miss a kiss." From the toad's point of view he was definitely right.

My Queen Bee, Jessica, was full of confidence, a successful entrepreneur, her business was expanding. There were functions for Lady Wendy Windblows and a luncheon to honour Sir Cumference etc. She had a very expensive car, and she seemed to like me. She was not working every night of the week, and sometimes, on returning her to her sumptuous flat, I would stay late, and it got later and later. She was wonderful.

Gayle would occupy my time and senses on the intervening nights and most Saturdays. She seemed to enjoy cooking, claiming that it was cheaper to eat at her place before we went out. She was full of opinions and feelings, talked a lot and listened more. I was staying later and later at her home too. She too was wonderful.

Granddad had also said that when it strikes twice the recipient was in trouble. Once and you don't know whether you are on your head or your heels: Second strike and you don't know if you are on this earth or 'Fullers' earth. But in both cases you were perpetually on cloud nine, again he was right.

Months went by with me having a most exciting social life.

One time Jessica had to organize a wedding function at the pad of the Marquis Dalrymple Chamonais. Preparations extended overnight and I was invited to stay there. I had been used to high living, but this was out of this world. Use of the heated pool; a horse-riding lesson; my first taste of Bolinger; Flunkies, foie *gras,* and truffles.

Then, on the other hand, Gayle could really brighten up an evening when just sitting in the dark.

They both began talking of me moving in. What was I going to do? I just had to give up this philandering. I had been introduced to, and approved by, both sets of parents. Gayle's were homely down to earth, 'Tha Knows' types.' Nothing much that they touched had ever turned to gold. That is except Gayle.

Jessica's parents obviously had some of the Midas genes. They were surrounded with opulence and their daughter was a jewel of rare price.

It was growing on me that I did favour one more than the other. But how could I tell the other? What would be the reaction?

More of Granddad's advice came flooding back, "There is no fury like a woman's scorn."

I was sure that he would be right. I would have to take anything that was coming to me. With any luck only one need know and would fly off the handle.

I determined to tell her that an earlier flame had come back into my life and I had found that the fire was still burning. I would not say that the fire had been raging out of control all the time I had known her. There would be some pleadings and perhaps anger but once begun it would have to be seen through to the end.

So I did it.

There I was nervously in the lounge of the Crown Plaza with Gayle. My body language must have told her something, for she asked what it was that was bothering me. I told her the story of my old flame and described Jessica. A handkerchief was drawn and a tear was wiped. There was much biting of lips.

I ventured, "I will not be 'moving in,' with you or you with me."

There were more tears, "I am sure that I love you more than she does." she sobbed.

"I have a feeling that it may be so," I said, "but, 'Que sera sera; whatever will be, will be."

I told her that my Granddad had, among his advices, said, "One of the most important facts about falling in love is that, 'It is just as easy to fall in love with a rich girl as it is to fall in love with a poor girl."

There was a flood of tears and another handkerchief. "Is that why you are not choosing me?" She asked between her sobs.

"Oh! No," I said leaning over to put a consoling arm around her shoulders, "Of all the advice he gave me, and he was always right, but on that bit of his advice he was definitely, but definitely, wrong."

We went into the restaurant to have our meal. It took some time for her to recover. When she had, and we were finishing our meal, I produced a small package and gave it to her to open.

She fumbled with the wrapper, and when she was just about to realise what the contents were, I said, "We will find a house, get married, and, for the first three weeks after our marriage I will expect you to go to bed wearing nothing, but 'La Nuit de Paco-Rabanne'."

*   *   *

LOOKING FOR JESUS

I'm looking for baby Jesus,
He's nowhere to be found.
But devotees of Bacchus,
Everywhere abound.

I cannot see the shining star,
Among the twinkling lights.
Although they are spectacular,
Like a million meteorites.

I cannot hear the angels sing,
When ghetto blaster's roar.
Or hear about the glad tiding,
That made the spirit soar.

There are no shepherds in the fields,
No Gabriel with his horn.
But plenty of so called wise men,
Whose wisdom seems stillborn?

A shed of battery hens I find,
When seeking for a stable.
Or a milking parlour,
With cows attached by cable.

I've found a Father Christmas,
In his sleigh with reindeers too.
He's advertising Tesco,
With his ho, ho, ho, halloo!

He can't be in a manger,
With stuff that those cows drop.
Midwife and social worker,
No doubt would blow their top.

Ah! here's a model Jesus,
Mary and Joseph and all.
Folk singing, "Hark!" and "Glory!"
And a donkey in a stall.

Everyone rejoicing,
With 'Happy Christmas' talk.
But if you mention Jesus,
They never walk the talk

I think I'll give up looking,
Go home to a feather bed.
They all know know't of Jesus,
I'll 'TELL' them tomorrow, instead.

THE WITCH FINDER

Once again there was trouble on the railway. Most of the office staff were late arriving but Harold, a young practical joker, cool, smart both in dress and brain, was in as usual, early. As the stragglers arrived and passed by they said a reluctant, "Good morning," to Harold and related the difficulties encountered on their way to the office. Some had been waiting in the cold, others having had to change to a bus route.

If they noticed, they did not comment but there was a besom standing at the corner by his desk.

Eventually, George, the oldest and most vociferous member of the staff, having related his tale of woe, noticed and commented on the besom, asking, "What is that?"

Oh! Harold replied, "It's a broomstick."

"But what is it doing here?" asked George.

"Well, that's a good question," said Harold with a sly smile and a touch of disdain, "You have just been moaning to me about the difficulties and discomfort you have had in travelling this morning, and that is my solution."

Those within hearing distance were well used to Harold's sassy humour. But Mary, though nobody knew it, had a crush on him. She enjoyed it even more. To her, he was one of those things which looked too good to be true, but he wasn't.

She herself was a classy 'dresser', and had a classy chassis which fitted perfectly into those dresses. She never seemed to have a hair out of place and her perpetual smile showed the place where a precision engineering dentist had done some of his best work.

"Very funny, very funny," said George, "I suppose you are now going to treat us to some black magic?"

"If that is what you would like, here have some." Harold opened his desk drawer and offered a box of 'Black Magic' chocolates to George. There were some loud chuckles and Harold offered the box of chocolates to his audience around the office.

Mindful that the supervisor had still to arrive and he would be in no mood for Harold's funnies, they settled down to concentrate on their work. That is, all except Mary. All morning she kept taking every opportunity, more than she usually took, to pass by Harold's desk. She never failed to get his tea for him, offer one of her biscuits and today ask him questions about the broom. She had never seen one, although she had always been fascinated by witches, Hob Goblins and Fairy stories.

At lunch break when most staff were out she noted that those who were still in the office were mostly heads down, occupied on their own business. One was cross-wording; another was running up the office phone bill by chatting incessantly to her boyfriend. This was evident by the way she was twisting and unconsciously fiddling with her hair whilst talking. George was peacefully dozing. She said to herself, 'Now you lot keep on minding your own business and don't pay any attention to me.' Nobody was paying attention to her when she went to sit at Harold's desk. This alone gave her a warm glow of pleasure. But she was keenly interested in that broom. She wondered just what it would be like to sit astride a broom. Was it heavy? She wondered and wondered. While wondering her fingers fiddled with his pen and straightened the papers in his 'In' tray. She slid open the desk draw and there was the box of 'Black Magic' chocolates. She convinced herself that if she took one he would not miss it. Lifting the lid of the box she found it was full. Only the top layer of paper was disturbed. She pondered that the staff must have eaten at least ten. She definitely had one, and yet she could see a complete top layer. Real magic she thought, but it couldn't be! It was another of Harold's tricks. She took a toffee one anyway. Then her thoughts went back to the broom. She left the seat and bravely touched the broom. With much foreboding she leaned it away from the desk. It seemed heavy. She held the stick end up with the twig bristles resting on the floor and put one leg over the stick. She thought to herself, "I wonder how witches made their brooms go up?" In her mind she tried to remember the witch stories of her nursery days and whether they could help with the now important question. Do they say, "lets fly?" Or perhaps, "Broomstick make the dust fly?" "Up Broomsticks, go Broomsticks, Broomsticks are go?" "Broomsticks fly?" or something else? Suddenly the broom was not heavy at all and the twiggy end, which had been resting on the floor, was lifting her up. She and the broom rose swiftly to the ceiling. As she did, she instinctively expected to bang her head on the ceiling but it seemed as though the ceiling was made of jelly. She sailed right through electric wires and fittings. In fact she was sure that her head was inside the ceiling. The broom veered around the room and for a few seconds out through the outer wall and into the boss's office. Lucky he is not in, she thought. On she went through an inner wall, across a corridor and back into her own office. All this time the few people still in the office seemed not to take any notice. It was as if she were invisible. She was afraid and shouted. "Help!" but nobody heard, or seemed to hear. She also shouted, "Stop!" and a lot of other words that one says when frightened, including "Mum!" But she must have uttered the right phrase, as the broom made a smooth landing. It came to rest ten yards from Harold's desk and she had to pull it back to its original position by his desk. Just as she got it there George coughed and woke himself up.

He, embarrassed, looked around the room and saw Mary just releasing her grip on the broom, "Thinking of going for a spin Mary?" he said.

"D . . . d don't be silly," she stuttered, while she walked over to him. She was sure that he had not seen her flying because he had not responded to her cries, but she thought he may have noticed that she was being deceptive. She was relieved to put some space between her and the broom.

Desperate to change the conversation she asked, "Do you fancy a fresh cup of tea before they all come back?"

She spent all afternoon in a dream, trying to figure out the rules of flying. What did she say? What did she do that made it rise and land when it did? She had said so much when she was flying through the office walls. When it was time to go home she would watch Harold's every move. If he was a real live 'Harry Potter' type she would definitely work her charms on him, bewitch him before he realised it and he was definitely going to be hers.

As it approached 4.30, most of the staff were making an early dart for home, all considering that the trains would be still dysfunctional. She pretended to have lots of filing which had to cleared, but was, as she had intended, watching Harold. When most had departed Harold picked up the broom.

Mary stopped her pretence of filing in her excitement and anticipation that he was going to fly on that broom. She said, "Wrap up well dear, fasten your seat belt and don't forget your flying helmet dear, if you are going for a spin."

Harold tried to make light of this and answered, "I didn't bring one. If you are staying late and get hungry, you know, there are some chocolates in my drawer, but can't stop, must fly."

He went out of the room with the besom and down the corridor to the toilet. Mary waited a long time. The cleaning ladies came and Mary waited until one of them went into the toilet to clean. She knew in her heart that the cleaner would not find Harold, he was by now at his home.

That night she fell asleep fantasising about Harold soaring off into the sky, wishing she were riding pillion. How high and fast could it go? What were the necessary instructions? The matter which really crowded her thoughts was how to broach the subject. She had her chatting up experience; she was quite adept at small talk and riposte, but it was unlikely to be of use. How, she wondered, could she make small talk about the merits and demerits of broom-stick flight?

Next day she received a message from Harold on her office computer:-

"My Dear"
It struck me this evening. I arrived home at nearly midnight. Since then I have been brooding and unsettled, toying with my laptop and acting like a besotted lovelorn loon, trying to compose this missive. I could do nothing. I hear nothing but your voice. I am like a fool since I heard you call me 'Dear.' I offended some friends this evening by 'dreaming away' and not participating in their discussion. I kept hearing your voice, not theirs. I now realise that I always refrain from aiming my disparaging humour in your direction. This is not my usual habit. I fancy that I would like to hold you in my arms; have your head upon my shoulder; and hear you call me 'dear' again. I will go to bed and hope that tomorrow you will reply. Write something to me. How do I sign off? Shall I say dear or with love? I will leave it blank, because right now I feel that my head is not wired up properly."

"Gotcher," she said to herself, and fired off a reply.

"Dear dear, dear, dear.
I never thought you would ask! While your defences are down and your head is in a spin, I would be delighted to go two rounds with you. (Of the park) Afterwards we might share an expensive two

for £10 at the Black Bull. You might then not find my voice so ensorceling.

Yours in anticipation, 'Dear.'

He replied,

"Dear Me, What is happening to me?

Forget me going two rounds with you, in the ring or in the park. I am already punch drunk, I will settle for the two for £10 tonight, 6.00pm. I can't wait."

And so they spent the evening at the Black Bull.

Harold was besotted but tried to explain his confusion and his e-mail. He said, "I knew that another chocolate had been taken, and on the way home, I could tell that someone had ridden on the broom."

"How could you ever know?" she asked.

"It was left in a sort of automatic mode," he said,"

"So," she puzzled, "how did you know that it was me?"

"I remembered that you were hanging about in the office and I deduced that you were waiting to see me leave the office." he said.

"So you are a Wizard like Harry Potter, you went to Hogwarts and all that?" she asked excitedly.

"Not quite, but you are also a witch, not quite like Hermione," he replied.

Mary nearly choked on her wine as she said, "Am I?" "Well," said Harold, as he became very serious, "you would not have been able to fly if you did not have 'The Gift'. He continued, "All over the world some people have 'The Gift,' It is a hereditary thing, passed down in families from sometime in the 17th century and before."

"And you think I have it?" Her face took on a 'wry expression', "If I had not flown on that broom I would say you are extracting the urine."

"I definitely know you have 'The Gift' or some part of it. Some part of it in which your forefathers were particularly gifted." Nodding, he said, "You have a spell on me now."

"You have had too much from that litre bottle," she chided. "You won't be fit to drive your car home."

"No problem," he said, with a double open-hand gesture. "I

will fly you home on the broom. I have it hidden."

"Somewhere, long ago in the 17th century all over Europe the presence of witches and their supposed wickedness attracted incredible attention. There were accusations and executions of the people accused of witchcraft. It was a mass hysteria. The Church had specially appointed men called 'Witch Finders'. Of course they had to find some witches or be out of a job. So they always found some. The people that were accused were tortured to make them confess and ultimately their broken bodies were burned at the stake. Many of those who had, 'The Gift,' fearfully denied having it and kept the fact from their children. Thus it lapsed into the world of myth, but it was and is still is there in the makeup of some of us. Just like birds and nest building, who shows them how? It is just there perhaps in their DNA.

J.K.Rowling collected some of those myths; some false; some true; embellished them, and created her stories. You know now that some are true, you know that we can pass through walls, like those in Potter's railway station, don't you? And there are academy places somewhat akin to Hogwarts."

By now there was no doubt that Mary believed the lot. She said, "Excuse the pun but I am spellbound."

Harold continued, "I am an emissary, a sort of secret agent of one such academy. I am out here like a missionary, looking for those who have inherited 'The Gift,' and bringing them back into the fold, so to speak. "Well," he asked, "are you convinced? Anyway it is getting late and your voice still holds that spell on me. I had better take you home."

"Would you still like my head on your shoulder?" she teased.

"I would like nothing more, you witch."

As they flew to her home, Mary as pillion, with her head on the back of his shoulder, her arms around him hanging on tightly, she shouted, "I think that I have discovered what my family's 'Gift' was."

"What was it then?"

"Is there a gift for making wishes come true?"

A day in my life? A day in my life. What is a **day** in my life? 60 million years ago a day, as they know it, was 20 of their hours long and eons before that it was a lot less. Anyway I have no nights. I know they say I separated the light from the dark but it is all in a day to me. I suppose they mean a day of theirs.

Now today, I wonder if the goings-on in this twenty-four hours, their today, would suit them as an insight into an average day in my 'life'. I suppose today will suit them? Today I have this meeting. I don't know why I got into this situation of allowing myself to be present at meetings.

I remember, well, in fact I can never forget, it all started when they began to talk. They started to give everything names. Before, everything was, 'A that' and as I was the only one considering that, or that, or that, I knew exactly what 'that' was. Some of them to this day use a variation of 'that' when they call something a 'Thingy' or a, 'What do you call it?'

Then they started to understand each other. That was because of the 'that,' they named 'Eve,' her, 'that' gave a name to an 'apple' and the, 'that' she called serpent. All Hell was let loose then. Well really, there was no one in Hell then, besides him. I tried to thwart this common understanding among them by making and giving them differing tongues. It was to no avail, they even gave names to their tongues; they have a glib tongue; a sharp tongue; a viper's tongue; and even a false tongue; or a smooth tongue. They banded together in gangs with their tongues, each gang hating all others, and 'Him', right down there, soon got a following. What with the Canaanites, Medes, Persians, Israelites, Jebusites, Girgashites, the Midianites, Egyptians etc, etc, etc. They all took to him. Very few came here and I almost had the place to myself. I invented thunderbolts and floods to coerce them, but some would always survive and it would all start again. In the end I had to succumb, and they now have 'Free will,' to choose whether to come here or go down there.

Then those Greeks: Socrates, Plato and Aristotle appeared. They started inventing and constructing words like honour, love, honesty and conscience. Things which were only in their heads and were never 'thats' or things at all. They created a name for these things that weren't things, they called them abstract. Yes, it started then. I picked up all the honour, love, honesty and conscience types, which I must admit are better than the duplicitous types. A short time after, it really got worse, a man named Thomas Moore came here. I think 'Him', right down there worked Tom and the others on to me. Thomas and his gang pitied their brothers who had chosen to go down there and plagued me to make things down below fair. They have some thought that I can do anything! Of course that place was never intended to be *fair*. So they set about trying to make out that this place up here is not fair. A gang came here headed by one called Ben Franklin, he and his mates had the idea that, "All men are equal" and another called Thomas Paine wanted equal rights for men, nothing was said about women. I ventured to point out that I had given them, 'The Fair Sex,' which they called women, but they were not interested in that kind of fairness. Then there was one called John Brown who, down there, had an objection to the keeping of black slaves. He came here and one called Ghandi, arrived. A guy named Kennedy has offered his services to mediate between 'Him,' right down there, and myself.

They all, to a man, or should I say to a soul, think that we should negotiate a covenant of peace between us. Him with the tail won't budge, and neither will I, but they say that for the good of the whole world, we two must make compromises and sacrifices. I was not aware of many of them making a genuine compromise while they lived in the middle. Most, excluding Gandhi, Brown and very few others always had an ulterior motive. Or wanted a quid pro quo!

As they cannot get their wishes one way, they are trying a different tack. They have now picked on me and want to have a meeting today about democracy up here. They claim that I should not necessarily hold my position in perpetuity but should subject myself to free elections at regular intervals and they have had some sly digs, using their word 'nepotism'. They say in their propaganda that I am a despot. They say that my post should be open to all, even Him, right down there.

Today will be taken up with a meeting. You should attend one. They go on and on and on and last an eternity.

I know that when they have voted me out, which they will because they are stupid and always vote for the shyster, it won't be long before they are saying, "GOD HELP US!"

THE CONTENTS OF MY FRIDGE

Right at the rear,
One can of beer.
There's some butter there that once fell upon the floor.
There's a little bit of fish,
Lying on a Pyrex dish.
All squeezed in to a fridge that's two point four.

One slice of ham,
Some of Sundays lamb.
There's a box of eggs that came from Tesco's store.
There's a bottle of Black Tower,
And some milk that's going sour.
All squeezed in to a fridge that's two point four.

One onion, whole,
A toad in its hole.
Half a tin of baked beans in the door.
There's a Brussels sprout or two,
And an Avocado too.
All squeezed in to a fridge that's two point four.

One yogurt pot,
Some Chilli that is hot.
A half cooked steak that we all thought was raw,
There's some Gorgonzola cheese,
That'll fairly make you sneeze.
All squeezed in to a fridge that's two point four.

One chicken wing,
A sausage on a string.
You can tell that I am not an herbivore.
I will clean it out for sure,
But it's such a tiresome chore.
With them all squeezed in to a fridge that's two point four.

*   *   *

A TURN AROUND

Constable Good of the County Constabulary had, over twenty years, tried hard to make sergeant, but promotion had passed him by. He was a devout Christian but his God had never seemed to favour him. During his time as a constable he had transgressed. He had envied the young whizz kids, who to his mind were all kid and very little whizz. Their promotion seemed to come without effort. Consequently, in addition to his embarrassing number 40, he had carried a large chip on his shoulder and a guilt complex. His chagrin was manifest in his aggressive control of his wife Alice and daughter Janet.

Before, and in some cases up until the end of, the war, fathers stood at the gate when their daughter returned from an evening entertainment. The young girl would dread being a fraction later than father had decreed. If there was any transgression father would not only chastise the daughter but also vent his displeasure on any male accompanying her. PC. Good persisted with this practice until his daughter was approaching her nineteenth birthday. This watchful supervision extended to rules about her mode of dress, and in particular to her long-standing school-days attachment to one named George.

Father persisted with his opinion that George was a ne'er-do-well. George had a criminal record. Father knew this because he had access to such information. He knew that George had attempted to steal two books from the library when aged fourteen.

Janet knew of this and protested that they were 'Mathematics for the Millions' and a science book. George had excused himself, telling Janet that he needed them to help him with homework. The school had only two copies of the books and other boys hogged them. He was from, 'The other side of the track'. And father taunted Janet with this fact, quoting it as evidence that George was undesirable. But, as is the case with true love, she set her face against her father's wishes and at the age of nineteen she became pregnant and married George.

Mother was no less ruled in her movements. What had started as a happy marriage after the war had now degenerated to a life of worry and fear. Mr Good constantly wanted updates on her whereabouts. She had taken a part time job as a dinner/playground lady. This was against his wishes but it gave her some freedom of movement.

On Janet's wedding day her father didn't attend the wedding, refusing to give her away. He insisted that her mother should cease any contact with her sinful daughter. Of course, to sever relations with her daughter at such a time was never going to happen and Alice surreptitiously maintained contact.

George, on the other hand had, not fallen by the wayside. After his tangle with the police his probation officer had nurtured George's academic prowess and actually acquired the two books that he had tried to steal and added several others. George, by the age of twenty one was an accomplished Marine Engineer.

Unknown to her husband, Mrs Good had every other Friday afternoon free and when it could be arranged, she would spend it with her daughter. She would, on rare occasions, drop any news items as though she had received them on the phone. Her husband would inevitably castigate her, but she bore this stoically.

One Friday she did not go to work but rang in to take a 'Sicky,' she went off to visit Janet and obtain an eighth month update on her grandchild's progress. Janet had other exciting news. George had been chosen to fly to Cannes where two very expensive yachts had collided. His employers had been asked to assess the damage of one for an insurance company. George and one of his bosses were out there living it up.

Just when mother was taking her third tea cake the house imploded. The walls of the house, front and side had buried them both. Firemen and ambulance men managed to extract them from the rubble and whisk them off to the local infirmary.

The house next door to Janet's had had some sort of gas leak and had exploded. The occupant was dead. Alice was relatively unhurt, having only a broken her arm. With Janet they were not quite sure. She had not lost the baby but she was unconscious.

Alice was cleaned up despite. Despite the dirt and dust she was reasonably presentable and allowed to go home, but she could not go by bus. She did not know which bus and she did not have a coat or a handbag. The thought of asking her husband for transport would be too much, so she decided to wait for Janet to recover. She patiently consumed copious free cups of tea and was rewarded with the good news that Janet had regained consciousness but would need to be in intensive care for a while. A transport charity man offered to take her home so having been assured that the baby and Janet were going to be all-right she picked up her courage and accepted.

Mrs Good, with her broken arm; some bruises, minus her coat and handbag and very apprehensive of what she might meet at home, tried to compose herself while being driven home.

She had long left off having faith but found herself saying mixed up prayers. Oh! God, when will we be there? I've never been in any car but my husband's in my life. What will I say to him? He will bring the wrath of his God down upon me. Why do the two people I love most have to be the two most headstrong in the world? Her getting herself pregnant and marrying George. Him with his Pentecostal righteousness, insisting that they were bound for hell. He hasn't spoken of her since Christmas, when she said the Housing Association had allocated the house. Janet and George were making a life for themselves. They were moving up, "On the right side of the track." She would show her dad he was wrong to more or less kick her out of his house. Thought he would frighten me into not seeing her, did he. I shall not care if you kick me out PC Good 4 nothing, if you've a mind. How could we contact George to tell him? His 'best man' at the wedding works with him. He might know but how do I contact him? Oh! We're here now, go and face him.

He was not as irate as she had expected, In fact he was rather cool when he saw her arm in a sling, "Where have you been? The school rang to ask how you were they said you had rung in and that you were sick, you hadn't been to school."

Not expecting him to remain cool when he learnt where she had been, she replied, "I've just got out of a kind gentleman's car."

"Why where you been, in someone else's car?" He was beginning to warm up.

Holding her arm up, she said, "At the hospital. If you hadn't noticed, I have a broken arm."

There was ever so small a chink of sympathy when he asked "What happened, how did you break your arm?"

Expecting the tirade she said, "I have been with Janet, I thought that she needed me".

"Behind my back!" The sympathy had evaporated. "Oh yes it must be her time now and you went to see her. You know what I said, 'she'll get no succour from here.' And you sneak off to her!"

"Yes, Janet did need me, and I went to their house this morning."
She said, "Yes, I thought I would ring in sick and I could be with her
today; to do a few things for her. It was just as well, because George
is away on business." The word business was said with a sneer. "Yes
business, He is doing well at his job. They are going up in the world;
he is away in Cannes examining some boat. But Janet is lying in the
intensive care in the hospital."

Mrs Good was getting up courage and raising her voice a little as
she said, "'PC Good 4 nothing,' you always said, George is going to be
a failure, but your God must have decided different."

With absolute calm in his voice and certain sympathy he asked,
Why is she in the intensive care, has she lost the baby?"

Surprised by his change of tone and did not refer to the baby as 'it'
or that thing, she said, "No they are both going to be alright," and began
to tell him of the days happenings. How they both lay under the rubble
until the firemen got them out. The wonderful nurses and doctors at
the hospital. The Good Samaritan who drove her home. She was lucky
having only some broken bones, no blood spilt, just a couple of bruises.

Forgetting his dictum he interrupted "Is she is still in there? What
is the matter with her? Is she injured?"

Alice reminded him, "You said that I was not to mention her in this
house ever again, so why do you want to know."

"Is she injured?" He insisted. "She must be if they kept her in. And
she has not lost the baby?"

"What is it to you? She retaliated; "You turned her out and said you
didn't want anything to do with her, ever again."

"Tell me woman! Is she hurt?" he said anxiously.

"Yes she is, she has not lost the baby, yet. But she has a broken leg
and a broken arm, as well as the broken heart that you gave her. George
does not know and won't be back from Cannes until seven o-clock
tomorrow night. I didn't want to leave her but I had to, and get back
to face you."

"You could have stayed," he said quietly.

"I was afraid that you would be boiling with Holy wrath when I
had been found out."

"Well I'm not am I?"

She thought this a different type of anger.

He continued thoughtfully, "This is bad. Her husband doesn't know that she is there. He needs to know, and she will want him to know when she comes round."

"And no way to contact him," she mused.

"Yes there is. Where does he work? You make some tea."

She told him, but noted that he still would not say 'George.'

She made the tea, glad to be given orders in this different way, she heard him speaking to a police colleague, asking for an emergency call out number. He came back for his tea and said it is sorted She wondered if he actually said the word George to anybody.

Between gulps of his tea he said, "Make some sandwiches or something and go back to be with her. It might be a long vigil, and while you do that I will get the car out."

As she climbed into the car with the victuals, her coat and a handbag, she said to him, "Thank you for allowing me to go to her, and when you go to church on Sunday I will be pleased to go with you, and not under duress."

*   *   *

THE FARMERS LOT

He had ploughed the field for his lifetime,
And scattered the seed at May-day time.
But the seeds did not have a chance to grow,
The field was gleaned by a big black crow.

He dragged the plough which was seven bladed,
Over the field that the crow had raided.
He continued though the light had faded,
The field was then with furrows braided.

His thoughts for the crow were not sublime,
As he sowed the seed for a second time.
When he wandered home in the moonlight glow,
His thoughts were to place, a new scare-crow

THE FORMATION OF THE WOMENS INSTITUTE

Some time in 1911 a group of ladies in the village of Gladstone came together to form the Gladstone branch of the Women's Institute.

This village of Gladstone was picturesque, typical of those shown on a chocolate box. A duck pond, white walled cottages with thatched roof, a stream, many outlying fields of rolling farmland and many ladies with an abundance of common sense.

They initially met in the village hall where they shared and demonstrated their prowess of country crafts. They also invited knowledgeable speakers from the world outside Gladstone.

The very first speaker that they invited was, Mr Roland Butter, his subject being the uses of lactose and concentrating on the science of making Yogurt, which is a 5000 year old Turkish craft. This speaker started them on the road to enlightenment, the like of which St Paul experienced on the road to 'domestos'.

Member numbers grew and within a few years the village hall became unsuitable for meetings of such a large and august body. The then committee, Madam President, Mrs Panjandrum; Secretary, Miss A Scribbler, Treasurer Mrs Moneypenny together with other committee members, Miss. Ruth Less, Miss Joe Viality and Mrs BE. Merry, inspired all with the will to fund raise and acquire their own hall. Their successful efforts drew people and funds from far and wide, putting Gladstone village firmly on the map. A sympathetic landowner, Sir Cumferance, donated land, and the hall was built.

What then should they do for the grand opening? Much discussion took place; the suggestion of a competition took most votes. There was already an annual village flower show and a cattle show in the next village two miles away, it must not clash with that. Eventually it was narrowed down to a jam-making challenge. No, 'a jam-making festival.' But some non jam-makers suggested that the main ingredients of jam making, the berries, should also be exhibited and prized. All agreed it should be an open competition and the rules were drawn up, especially the requirements of the, to be exhibited, berries. Ten raspberries or ten loganberries all equally sized on a plate. likewise gooseberries, bilberries, cranberries and elderberries. The inclusion of strawberries, currants and even grapes, though not strictly berries were also included. It was such an enormous success and a great fund-raiser that it was agreed to make it an annual affair. Later it was further extended to include anything that could be produced from the berries as well as the jam. This included cordials, jellies and wine, which was very popular.

As the years passed it then metamorphosed into an annual berry festival, drawing large crowds of visitors to this, now well-publicised, village.

We are now in the year 2011, one hundred years have passed, today it is very common to have a speaker on Interstellar Travel, and the common tendency to fast food is staunchly shunned; but nudity has made an entry. Yes, the Gladstone Women's Institute has gone from strength to strength and so has **The Gladstone Berry Festival.** Even you must have heard of it?

FIDUCIARY HUBRIS

We can't have Christmastime this year,
We must dispense with Yuletide cheer.
They've made our money disappear,
We've not enough to buy a beer.

The men with all the banking brain,
Protest when governments constrain.
That their profession is arcane,
While they practise legerdemain.

To folk who had not means to pay,
Like those who only lived to play.
Bankers lent and they made hay,
No thought of a future rainy day.

Nemesis played her fickle game,
There was much claim and counter claim.
Politicians mouthed ne'er again, again,
Bankers sought to avoid disdain.

Consumed with avarice, and rash,
They said, "We're sorry we've lost your cash."
Excused themselves with such panache,
Lined their pockets and made a dash.

MAKING THE TEN COMMANDMENTS

Scene, a frosty morning on Mount Sinai. Present, God and Moses

Moses. Good morning God. You made it a cold night. As a matter of fact the last 30 nights have been cold. How was it for you? Where do you sleep? Would it be too much to ask you for one of your burning bushes to keep me warm tonight?

God. I'll think about it. I called you up here to give you the hard copy of all those commandments that your people heard on my tannoy a month ago. I did not bring you here to sit around in comparative comfort, and when you get back down there, you make them realise that there is no space up here for anyone who does not keep these commandments.

Moses. Yes that was a month ago. You have been burning your finger into these stones for 30 days. Couldn't you have given me some you prepared earlier? And why are they in Aramaic when we all speak Egyptian?

God. I could have given you some of what will be called the Dead Sea Scrolls but I am not going to help write them for another 700 years. These have got to be written on stone because I haven't shown you how to make paper yet. Let's get back to work or you will be here more than the standard 40 days and 40 nights. Where were we up to?

Moses. We had just finished, Thou shall not kill.

God. Ah yes.

Moses. The next one, Adultery, could I suggest an amendment.

God. SUGGEST AN AMENDMENT?

Moses. Well really. Strike it out altogether.

God. STRIKE IT OUT ALL TOGETHER? It is the main one! It is the one which none of you will keep, and it will make sure that heaven does not get cluttered up with mere mortals. I know that there are many rooms in my mansion but I've got to give you all a hurdle to get your leg over.

Moses. I've got to hand it to you God. Your plan is working well. Abraham sorted out Hagar, his wife's maid. And his wife couldn't see his side of the problem. So out of kindness she kicked Hagar and the baby out into the desert to starve.

God. Abraham was one of my chosen, who will populate the earth.

	His progeny will be as numerous as the grains of the sand.
Moses.	He made a good start and a good profit out of selling his wife's favours to the Egyptians. She probably started the oldest profession in the world. Then there was his brother Lot, who sorted out his two daughters. Did you forgive Lot's sin because he was drunk?
God.	It was all part of my master plan, right from Adam and the apple. I have a plan which you mortals will never understand.
Moses.	Try me! Would it spoil this vast, eternal plan if we strike out number 7? Even Jacob didn't knock out all those 12 sons and, only YOU know how many daughters, from just two wives. He had the services of his wife's maidservants to increase his production.
God.	NO! Seven is in. I'm even going to make an adjunct rule that, "He who looketh upon a woman to lust after her, will have committed adultery in his heart without even realising it." I also have an idea of making more than two sexes, sort of half sexes. That will make more trouble for you mortals.
Moses.	It looks as though you have the odds definitely stacked against us men. I note you don't say 'she' who looketh.
God.	Yes I get more fun out of tormenting man with this adultery than I get from chucking a few thunderbolts about, although making an earthquake or a flood is quite humorous.
Moses.	Adultery is one of the best things in our miserable lives and you have to make it illegal.
God.	Yes, I know, it is one of the best things.
Moses.	Unmarried women are the only ones who will qualify. Heaven will be full of women who have, in your words, 'Not known a man.'
God.	Quite so! I have fixed it such that only virgins, as they will come to be called, can make it to heaven and I have developed a penchant for virgins. I have a future, most confusing, master plan for one of them. She will have it off with a ghost. Or at least she will say it was a ghost.
Moses.	Got it God. The shekel has just dropped. You made man in your own image, Therefore SEVEN HAS GOT TO STAY IN, For God's Sake!

A lady taxi driver arrives at No. 14 Prince Albert Avenue to pick up her fare. She is about to turn into the crunchy drive of number 14 when she is stopped at the gate by her customer.

Surprised to find a woman driver and a good looker he climbs into the back seat saying, "65 Westcott Drive please." and continues, "I hope your driving is as good as you look.

The driver acknowledges the address thinking, he didn't take long to make a pass, and she begins to drive off. She has not driven far when she answers to his question. "I have an advanced drivers licence and it is clean and in case my driving brings on an attack of the vapours, for such an emergency I have a first aid box." She pauses, and then continues, "This is a very salubrious neighbourhood, do you live here?"

"No," he replies, "Just visiting a friend", and being self confident, he continues "A lady friend to be exact."

"A lady friend? Gentlemen visit their lady friends for supper; they visit their mothers for afternoon tea."

"She is a lady friend," he said and being emboldened added, "I sometimes take afternoon tea with her three times a week or sometimes take morning coffee."

"She must make a very good cup of tea?"

"She does that, she is an excellent tea maker."

Moving the conversation up a step the driver ventured, "I suppose she is an even better morning coffee maker?"

"Yes" said the passenger, "her morning coffee is better than her afternoon tea."

The driver fearing that she was getting embroiled tried to bring the conversation down, "I think I had better change the subject, we are moving into the wink, wink nudge, nudge area."

The passenger, full of bravado continues, "The usual guy who picks me up understands the situation and plays it cool."

"I am sorry," she says, "I am new to this taxi driving, so new, I started this morning and you are only my fifth fare. I understood that taxi drivers always engage in conversation with their passengers."

"Usually they do," he said, "so you would be wise to brush up your conversational skills. Geographical knowledge is good, especially on the way to an airport."

Approaching Westcott Drive she announces, "Here we are at Westcott Drive, what number did you say?"

"Number 65 and what have you got on your clock?"

"Three pounds fifty." she said.

When the car stops he opens the door and steps out, but leans through the now open window to hand her four pounds saying, "Keep the change."

Before he has withdrawn his hand she very slowly moves off saying, "Thanks, and to add a little more to our conversation, I can tell you that my brother lives at 14 Prince Albert Avenue and he is six foot three tall. Thanks for the tip." And she moves off at speed.

*   *   *

Move over Shakespeare I've written a sonnet.

THE UNSPOKEN LOVE

I never hear you say that you love me,
Though that you do is plain for all to see.
They can see it burns just like a great fusee
But please, could you not whisper it to me?

My love for you would reach up to the skies,
Of you my love I shout and lionise.
You are the one that I would canonize,
But speak, my love, lest love should fossilise.

If you, by chance, could voice a word of love,
I could rejoice as angels from above.
Yet, being sure that if push comes to shove,
Yours is the love that I am thankful of.

You'll always love me and we'll never part,
I feel this in my bones and in my heart.

Inspector Roddington's, thoughts tossed and turned as his brain went over and over the facts trying to evaluate possible explanations. Did Basher possess supernatural powers? If so, why had he not used them before? Roddington had a long association with Basher. He could hear the words of the latest conviction, "Joseph Bashall, although your crime this time seems trivial, I am swayed by Detective Roddington's request that you be given a custodial sentence. I have therefore decided that you spend the next six months in one of Her Majesty's prisons." That was when he was only a detective. Basher's 'collar', would help toward his promotion. With Roddington any 'collar,' was welcome towards promotion. Basher had found a wallet containing eleven pounds and had not reported his find to the police. His crime was 'Stealing with intent to deprive.'

Roddington was now nursing his own personal wrath and grief reflecting that he had been a bit of a 'shit.' He had insisted on a custodial sentence for only eleven pounds, which was very hard on Basher who, partly as a consequence, had just spent two months in hospital. Roddington was now a little remorseful and thought his action had been a bit mean-spirited.

Basher had found the wallet, thought it a bit of luck, and spent most of the money on drink. Rolling home he had attempted to cross the road on a pedestrian crossing and was knocked down by a car which happened to be driven by a policeman.

While in hospital Basher, with the aid of a solicitor, had tried to claim compensation, but had failed because Roddington, had produced witnesses that claimed Basher was not on the crossing and was in fact drunk at the time.

On leaving the hospital Basher had sought out the policeman as he came off duty. He said, "You lied over me not being on the crossing," then he pointed his finger at the policeman's head, almost touching it, and said, with his finger pointing as if it was a gun, "PC.241 you're dead."

The policeman, thinking that Basher was again drunk, passed the matter off knowing that Roddington had by then found the source of Basher's eleven pound wealth and was about to arrest him.

Three weeks later, on Basher's first full day behind bars, the policeman was chasing a burglar over a roof and PC 241 fell to his death. The Coroner's verdict was accidental death, but rumours abounded that it was the effect of Basher's curse.

Roddington was not deaf to the rumours and they tore into his mind. Perhaps Basher had some sort of power. Perhaps it was his doing. Basher had been as straight as an arrow since coming out of prison, seemingly tea-total. Although he did not have any obvious employment he was becoming socially acceptable. Thinking about the possibility of unnatural powers and nursing burning desire for revenge, Roddington considered that whatever Basher thought of him, he had to find out; he had to go and find Basher.

It was not difficult; Basher's favourite haunt was now the civic café at the civic centre and not the pub.

Basher, who hated Roddington, saw him coming and opened in a satirical tone, "Good morning Inspector, Roddington. I won't ask how you're doing, I've heard of your promotion and your troubles, I'm not sorry for you and in case you ask me, I'm doing nicely, thank you."

After some acrimonious talk of old times, Roddington broached the subject. "People still talk about your curse on that fellow Blake and how they think you have mystic powers."

"Have you come to put me away for what people say? You should be trying to get the kid who ran your daughter down and put him away, you found it easy enough to bang me up over eleven pounds and a wallet."

"That's not easy," said Roddington, "I know all about him, he was a 'Joy Rider' and in the circumstances I was taken off the case. He got off with a, 'Slap on the wrist and don't do it again,' sentence. I would have built the case up to get him at least 15 years. I would have sent him up for stealing a car; driving without a licence; driving without insurance and I could have added, without due care and attention. That's without manslaughter of my daughter."

A wry smile appeared on Basher's face as he said, "It's nice to know that you can be screwed up by the same law that banged me up with the screws."

"Yes," Roddington made an acknowledging nod, "the law is not always fair and I must admit it."

"In my case," Basher ventured, "PC Blake got his comeuppance because I put the spell on him."

"Don't try to convince me that you really can cause misfortune to befall people with your curses," said Roddington, while all the time hoping that Basher could. He continued trying to draw Basher out. Drawing information out of people was his profession; he had done it with hundreds of criminals.

Basher retained his aggressive mode, "I don't give a monkey's what you think I can or can't do, but Blake got his didn't he?"

Roddingtons real intentions showed, "I wish I could do the same to that sod who killed my Gillian."

"I get it," Basher's eyes lit up. "You've come here to see if I can do it. You want me to do it for you?" He pointed his finger at Boddingtons's head and touched it, just as he had done with Blake, and said, "You want me to put the finger on that kid, and say you're dead don't you?"

"If only you could, if only it was some power that you have?" Roddington breathed.

"Since I got that bang on the head, and you did me out of the compensation by sticking up for Blake, lots of funny things have happened."

"Funny things?" enquired Roddington.

"I had a tip for a horse and came to the library next door to look at its form in the papers. The girl in the library saw me and said that she remembered me; I was the man who, a year ago, was knocked off the zebra crossing. She said that she spoke to you but you did not use her as a witness."

Roddington knew the tactics to use in such situations. Say nothing, it will pass, the other fellow will resume talking.

Basher did resume, "We talked over a cup of tea in here, I didn't fancy the horse but she is a bit superstitious and she wanted to back it saying that it was providence. Said she had never backed a horse before, I had to put the pound on for her. Then it came in fifty to one. She bought me a steak dinner in here out of the winnings. Then she said that my name, 'Bashall' was interesting, said it came from Lancashire. She did a bit of study on my family tree. We are quite friendly, I see her here nearly every day, and bugger me if she didn't get five numbers up, netted 1,260 quid."

Roddington interrupted, "Lucky girl, but surely it was

coincidence, that if she got good luck for helping you, I get such bad luck for harassing you?"

"Nar, I had nothing to do with that, as you say it was coincidence, wasn't it?"

With a thoughtful look and a nod of his head, Roddington conceded, "Yes it was, I suppose it was."

"Yes but the girl in the library found out that my family come from a place called Bashall in Lancashire. We went up there, her and me. I think she fancies me. She told me that there were a lot of witches up there at one time."

"So you are descended from a witch are you?"

"I don't know but things are queer," mused Basher.

"If you were, you could boil a few frogs legs and cast a spell for me," Roddington joked.

"I would not! More likely I would cast one on you, for the way you treated me in the past. Anyway you don't boil frogs legs or stick pins into dolls."

Roddington became excited, "If you are sure of what you don't do, then you must have an idea of what you should do?"

"If I did, what's in it for me?"

"If you could do it, if you could do that, it would be worth a lot of money to me."

Basher took him seriously, "Would it be worth five grand?"

"A bit steep isn't it," Roddington said sheepishly.

Basher was in business mode and Roddington was beginning to believe that he really had some sort of supernatural power to actually make it happen.

"I don't think so," said Basher with confidence, "Three grand that you did me out of as compensation, and two for the job," he continued with a taunt, "I can see you being worth much more than that."

Roddington frowned. "I am not worth much more than that but it would be good to see the job done."

"Write a cheque for five grand and I'll try," said Basher.

Roddington took out his cheque book to write the cheque.

Basher played along with him, "You're serious about this aren't you? Don't put a date on it; I'll cash it when and if it happens."

As Basher put the cheque into his pocket he taunted Roddington again, "If it doesn't happen and I cash this cheque you will not be able to get me because you have just entered into an illegal contract and you can't stop it because it is an offence to issue cheques which you have no intention of honouring."

"I would get you another way," said Roddington confidently.

"I'll bet you would," countered Basher, "but you will not be bothered if or when I cash it. Where does the victim live?"

Roddington slid a folded piece of paper to Basher and said, "I really believe you can do it."

"When it happens, "Inspector" you will be on cloud nine."

"Something near," said Roddington.

A week later, Basher sought out the joy rider. Pointing to the lad's head he uttered the words, "You killed Roddington's kid, you are finished. He will get you, you are as good as dead, you are dead."

A month later Roddington was driving his Mercedes when he received a call about a bank raid in Main Street. He drove there, siren blaring. It was indeed a bank hold up. He arrived in time to see the get-away car drive away. He gave chase, being confident that a Mégane could not outrun his Mercedes. It was soon evident to the fugitives that a Mercedes with a bellowing siren was following them and they increased their speed. Roddington did likewise.

After many turns and twists Roddington could see that there was a long vehicle obstructing the path of the Mégane and, at the same time, other oncoming traffic blocked the oncoming lane. Not being able to proceed, the getaway car suddenly stopped. Roddington was within feet of it. He instinctively steered away from it. But he steered his Mercedes to the right, straight into the path of the on-coming car. There was one almighty crash as two vehicles became one. The occupants of the Mégane sped off on foot from their car, both were unscathed. One of them looked very much like Basher but, after many police requests for witnesses, none came forward. Strangely nobody had noticed the Mégane making a sudden stop or two people alighting from it, as all eyes had been on the tangled Mercedes and it's unfortunate driver.

There were two fatalities due to the crash that day. Both had died instantly. One was Roddington. The other, after identification, happened to be a joy rider, whose joy had ceased abruptly when he chose to tangle with Roddington's Mercedes.

It was ironic in the way Roddington had in fact achieved his revenge. The local newspapers were full of the gory details. They made many column inches of the coincidental links between Roddington, his daughter and the Joy Rider. The Joy Rider had only recently escaped custodial punishment for running down Miss Roddington. He was on probation and banned from driving.

Roddington as it happened, was insured for a tidy sum and his estate was easily enough to cover Basher's fee. The cheque was tendered within an hour of the mishap. Unfortunately Roddington was not aware of it. He was 'Over the moon,' having well passed cloud nine.

*   *   *

GRANDMA'S TREASURES

The other day,
Gran passed away,
You have to clear the house, when one deceases.
The aspidistra in a pot,
And silk dress that was shot,
Some of Grandma's, treasured bits and pieces.

Granddads trilby hat,
An iron that was flat,
A piece of cheese that had been chewed by 'Meeses'.
There's a porcelain collie dog,
And a knitted golliwog,
Some of Grandma's, treasured bits and pieces.

One diamond ring,
Some pearls upon a string,
She said that she would leave them to the nieces.
There was a vase she said was Ming,
But I dropped the bloomin' thing,
Gone was one of Grandma's bits and pieces.

A nineteen sixties frock,
A cuckoo in a clock,
A selection of Tesco mini cheeses.
Towels hanging on the door,
And a robe she never wore,
Some of Grandma's, treasured bits and pieces.

Scrabble in a box,
A fur from off a fox,
And some Jif she often used with elbow greases.
There's some awful long legged boots,
Curtains made from parachutes,
Some of Grandma's, treasured bits and pieces.

A coronation cup,
A stool for a hop up,
Some rouge she used to rub upon her cheekses.
There's an old sewing machine,
That she got when aged eighteen,
Some of Grandma's, treasured bits and pieces.

A box of Granddad's tools,
A set of carpet boules,
And some medicine to ward of all diseases.
A keyboard played by ear.
Many songs of yesteryear,
Some of Grandma's, treasured bits and pieces.

We got the auction man,
An antiquarian,
He looked in all the cracks, and all the niches.
He offered money on the spot,
And he'd take the bloomin lot,
All of Grandma's, treasured bits and pieces.

Marian was 23 years old and married happily, indeed very happily to the man of her dreams. That was until ten minutes earlier when a cloud had appeared on the horizon. She was nursing her three-month old son and had suddenly remembered a fortune telling session where she had been given an envelope to hold for a year. She had just opened it and found a worrying prediction. It had been given to her when she was hosting seven of her best friends, all of whom were grammar school alumni.

These Grammar School friends had regular reunions which had been nights out on the town. The socialising continued when they were at University and when putting their feet on the first rung of the ladder of success.

As they climbed the ladder and found husbands, their get-togethers became, "Who is the hostess with the mostest." They had exhausted the 'Grand tour,' of each newly acquired home and the ooh, aahs, which surround any new-born. A year ago, on one of her get-togethers, Marian had invited a clairvoyant, one Madame Zara.

A long time before that, as part of the group's revels to celebrate 'A' level successes, they had visited this same Madame Zara, to see what the cards foretold for them. Much giggling had ensued with the various Tarot predictions which, in particular, singled out Marian as the only one at that time who was not in any way smitten with a member of the opposite sex. The prediction was that she would, as the cliché says, 'Know him when she sees him,' it would be love at first sight. When he came along he would be constantly true and love her forever, definitely till death you do part. He would be very successful in his chosen profession. In fact his ladder of success would be lying flat on the ground such that he would not have to climb it. They would have two boy children.

That week it so happened that the local boy's grammar school had arranged a disco to celebrate their successes and wish each other bon voyage as they prepared to go their separate ways in the world. The local grammar school girls were invited, which, of course, included Marian's coterie.

During this evening there were some eulogies. Boys' were praised for their sporting prowess, social and academic ability and the general all round good chaps that they were. The head boy,

James, did his bit of eulogizing, praising the masters and the school. That's when it happened. He was the one that Madam Zara had seen, Marian was sure of it. Telling her friends started a major match making project to engineer an introduction. The result was inevitable because Marian is still a good-looker to this day.

Years passed, with marriages, new houses and children, Madame Zara's first Tarot predictions were ostensibly fulfilled. The girls, now ladies, had again invited Zara, and Marian was given a second prediction, which told her. "You are pregnant."

"No I am not, I am not. We planned to wait for two years."

"Nevertheless you are, but since you are not of a mind to believe, I will not tell you what else I see, but will write it down and put it in an envelope for you to read one year from now."

The year had passed, during which Marian did have a boy child. James and Marian had a slight disagreement on the name that the boy should be given. She wanted it to be James, but he wanted it to have the name of the child's grandfather Joseph. It was resolved that it should be Joseph and James went to register the birth.

On his return he confessed that he had given in to her request and after all registered the birth name as James.

Miriam opened the letter. Madam Zara had written, 'Though you do not believe you are pregnant, by the time you read this note you will have borne a boy. This boy will have all the world can give him until his fourteenth year. The cards do not tell me anything beyond his fourteenth year. You will call the child James after his father.'

What could it mean? Marian pondered while holding her three-month old baby to her breast. Her son would enjoy his young life to the full. Why would Madam Zara not, or could she not, say what sort of teens or manhood he would enjoy? In fact she had said that beyond the year of fourteen, the cards told her nothing. Perhaps her son was not going to reach his teens? No! That was too awful to contemplate, but she did contemplate. "If that is what the card, the ten of cups foretold," she said to the child, "then you will have the best of lives until then." Marian eventually convinced herself, that should it be the case that he was to have a short life, then she would give him the best.

Breast milk, all the pundits said, was the best for babies. Nature intended cow's milk for calves. She consumed the latest proprietary, post natal, food supplements that claimed to enhance the quality of her milk and although they tasted foul, she persisted for junior's sake. As he grew there was no child in the country who had more teddies and gizmos. By his fifth birthday, he acquired all the latest, 'must haves' for precocious kids. All whims were indulged. There was little heed of safety, as his demise was scheduled for the fourteenth birthday or near. What could happen in the interregnum? Something that she never expected happened and caused much heartache. Her husband began to object to her indulging the boy's whims such that they began to argue.

In consequence the boy grew up to be short on concentration and long on bad tempers. Later still, he was given his own television, DVD player, X-box, bicycle, skateboard and skiing holidays.

As the boy grew in size, bullying, selfishness and pugilism became the norm, often even venting his temper on his mother, lashing out with his fist or foot.

In desperation, Marian's husband had reluctantly left her rather than continue with the constant bickering over the boy's bad behaviour. The cards had not foretold that. They had foreseen a love lasting forever. Zara seemed to be wrong. Could she be wrong on other parts of her prophecy?

At school, teachers were equal recipients of the aggressive behaviour. James' short attention span caused him to lag behind his peers in academic ability. This, and later truancy, caused Marian much heartache and apologetic dialogue with the school authorities. Nevertheless he was her son, with the sword of Damocles, or the Ace of Swords hanging over him. She loved him and had resolved to make his short life as happy as she possibly could. To all who complained she stoically accepted and defended his atrocious behaviour.

Eventually his 14th birthday came and went. Marian became more and more anxious, expecting James to be, struck down with some terminal illness or disease like typhoid or meningitis. Maybe it would be some rare contagion like Green Monkey disease.

A month passed and another. James' tantrums were continuing. Lying awake at night in her lonely bed she thought, could the cards have been wrong? Was she a fool for believing them? They were wrong about her husband's devotion to her forever. What if?

James had started staying out late at nights and, although he would not say where he had been or what he had been doing, a visit from the police gave her the answer. The police alleged that the boy had been stealing cars and joy-riding. They had no definite proof but they were quite sure he was stealing. She had endured what she was now considering to be the torment of James' warped personality and now this. Had her doting and tolerant attitude wasted fourteen years? She had mistakenly bred a brat who was almost uncontrollable.

One night while lying in bed, anxiously worrying where he was and what was he doing, the police called again. This time they were not alleging, but were positive he had stolen a car and crashed it into another car. He had not survived.

They told Marian that the occupant of the other car, a lady, was also killed. Her name was Sarah Clitheroe. She had been some sort of clairvoyant. Amid the shock and tears, Marian thought, 'Sarah', could this lady have been Madame Zara?

Marian consoled herself by thinking that the cards in their twisted way had been correct. It was Madame Zara in the accident. She was not a Romanian as she had told people. She was an ordinary Lancashire lass. This explained why she had not been able to see beyond James's 14th birthday.

Marian also considered that she was right to have permitted James to be happy in his way, although it had sometimes been hell for her and she had sacrificed her husband for him.

On the day of James's cremation, as Marian was driven to the crematorium, there was only sadness and tears. She knew that all her acquaintances would be nursing derogatory thoughts of James and his anti-social behaviour. Nevertheless her old friends outwardly commiserated and went through the customary hugging after the ceremony. She had not played host to them for years and had made excuses for her absence when invited by others. Out of the blue, and through the tears came a hug of a different kind, which persisted for many minutes. It was the hug of her husband James.

When he broke his grip she said with even more tears, "I suppose your sentiments are, 'I told you so'?"

"Not so," he replied grabbing her again, "You did what you did for him because you loved him. I could not love him in the same way. I've missed you both, but Oh! How I missed you.

These words accompanied by the embraces and tears seemed to

meliorate the heartache. When all the friends who were invited back to her home for the finger food, were departing, Marian implored James to stay longer. After they had all gone she fell upon him, hanging about his neck, there were more and more hugs and messages that could not be conveyed in words.

After a while she ventured to ask," Will you come back to this house, I need you and have always needed you. I need you terribly now."

James, hearing some words that he was longing to hear, ventured, "If I come back, will you give up your addiction to looking into the future?"

"Oh! no, oh no!" She replied.

James, taken aback, said, "I think you should, after all the terrible things that have beset you. How can you possibly believe that they had anything to do with Zara's mumblings? Do you really believe that the future can be foreseen?"

"Oh yes, she said, "I do believe it, implicitly. All the things she foretold have come to pass except two."

"Here we go again! And which two are they?" he asked.

"Zara said that you would love me forever. Do you think you will?"

"I have loved you ever since we first met at school and I have loved you all the time you had those silly notions about Zara. Despite all that has happened and what I still consider to be your persistent foolish beliefs, I cannot help myself. There's not a bit of doubt about the enduring and deep love that I have for you." was his reply.

Amid more tears and snuffling she managed to say, "You have no idea how much that eases the pain but there is still one unfulfilled Zara prophesy which has still to happen."

"What is it? I suppose you feel it is inevitable," said James.

"Yes I hope it is inevitable," Marian positively enthused, "Zara said I would have two sons, and I sincerely hope she was right."

DINNER FOR TWO

He arrives home rather later than usual. > > > > >

HIM.   Hello dear, sorry I am a bit late; I've had a pig of a day.

HER.   Bad day or not, now that you are here, hurry; get.rid of the five o-clock shadow and get yourself decently dressed, we are eating out.

HIM.   Isn't it a bit cold to eat outside?

HER.   Very funny, now get ready we are eating at 'Les Dearoh'.

HIM.   Havens! That's a bit above our class isn't it?"

HER.   "Maybe, but don't worry, I'm paying.

Later after he has dressed > > > > > >> > > > > > > >

HIM.   OK. How do I look?

HER.   Do you ever consider that you may be sartorially dyslexic? With that tie you will blind the waiters.

HIM.   Then the tie will be an asset. They won't be able to read the bill.

HER.   Go and get another, more sober one, before I over tighten that one for you, and hurry up, we're booked in for 6.30. To-night, not tomorrow!

Later after she is impatiently waited for him to return > > > >

HIM.   How now?

HER.   That's better, though not much, but where have you been? It's 6.30 now; we are late. Let's get in the car and go.

In the car > > > > > > > >> > > > > > > > >> >

HER.   Is there something wrong with the car? Why are you driving so slowly? We should be there by now.

HIM.   No nothing amiss with the car, but I am not sure of the way. It's not like I'm a regular client at this place.

HER.   Oh, for god's sake turn left here.

HER.   Now left again.

HER.   Right at the next and it's on the left. Even you can't miss it.

HIM.   It's a good job you knew where this place is or we would have been driving around till closing time. God! The car park is full, look that's a Roller over there taking up two bays, and there are four 'Mercs' on this side.

After parking the car. > > > > > > >

HER. For a male who is supposed to be superior to us poor females, the way you were driving and parking, I wouldn't be surprised if it is closing time.

HIM. Let's get in. Here's the maître de coming to greet us.>> Good evening, We have a reservation. Sorry we're late. Navigation problems.

WAITER. "The time is no problem sir. Would you like to go straight to your table?

HER. Yes please.

HIM. Good job you said that; an aperitif here would cost an arm and a leg Then I would not have been able to lift it to my lips even if I could balance on one leg. Just look at the silverware on these tables! More stuff on one table than you have in our cutlery drawer.

HER. Well! One thing is for certain, you won't be eating your chips with your fingers.

HIM. Wow! Look at the size of the serviettes! How do they distinguish them from table cloths? By the pattern I suppose.

HER. They will prevent you from slopping down that tie of yours. I'm glad I don't have the job of washing them, imagine me ironing this lot.

HIM. Let's take a look at this tome of a menu. Jesus! Look at the prices. We will need two cards to pay for this lot. I know a restaurant where we could have eaten dirt cheap.

HER. That will be where you eat with the lads after the match, but we don't want to eat dirt, however cheap it is. That's why we are here. I'm trying to give a Philistine like you a bit of culture. What are you considering from the menu?

HIM. I was thinking of having a burger.

HER. A burger? Don't you want to choose something you haven't had before? Anyway an Italian chef might not know how to cook a burger.

HIM. He must do, there's one on the menu and I've never had a £9 burger before."

HER. Don't tell such porkies. There are no burgers on the menu it's not that sort of place.

HIM. Would you look at that, steak on a stone, I wonder what you get for that? And look at the price, can you afford it? It won't cause a run on your bank, will it?

HER. If that is what you want, have it, whatever it is. It must be steak of some kind and you like your steak.

HIM. What do we do if the wine waiter comes offering his wares?

HER. Don't worry ask for house wine.

HIM. At these prices I'll ask him how much they charge for water. Or shall we have one glass of table wine, between the two of us.

HIM. Here's the waiter 'Señor Straccaciatella' now, have you got enough strength to order?

WAITER. Madam are you ready to order?

HER. I'll have the stuffed mushrooms and Tornados Rossini please.

WAITER. A very good choice madam, if I may say so, and how would you like it madam?

HER. Medium please.

WAITER. Excellent Madam, and for you sir?

HIM. I'll have this, here on the menu, and then steak on a stone.

WAITER. Thank you sir. Madam. Will you be requiring wine sir?

HIM. Er! Yes please two glasses of medium, white, house wine.

Time passes while waiting for service > > > > > > >

HER. When you ordered the soup, what kind is it?

HIM. I picked the one, 'Soup Dejour' we have had that before and it tasted nice.

HER. That means soup of the day or chef's choice and you know it. Why didn't you ask what kind it was?

HIM. It doesn't matter. It is cheaper than your stuffed mushrooms and the other option was Bisque d Homard.

HIM. He didn't ask how I like my steak.

HER. I'd give it to you straight through your heart.

HIM. Here's the wine; I daren't look at the price, look at the size of the glasses! Half a gallon in each.

HER. Half a gallon shouldn't bother you. You shift twice that when you are out with those drunken friends of yours. Anyway it tastes nice. Forget the price, let's enjoy it.

HIM. It does doesn't it, I am just beginning to like this place, I'll just start to nibble the bread till the soup comes.

HER. It's coming now. The soup is for him, the mushrooms are mine. Thank you.

HIM. Are you allowed to slurp your soup in a place like this?

HER. No, you are only allowed to slurp where you learnt the habit, at your Mum's table and tonight, when we come to the coffee you can't dunk either.

HIM. That was below the belt, boys always like slurping their soup.

HER. What is it like? Anyway, my mushrooms are gorgeous.

HIM. It's great. I think the chef would call it enthusiastic soup.

HER. Why?

HIM. I think he's put everything he had into it. A whole lobster at least.

HER. I thought you ordered the soup of the day? Have you got the Bisque, Lobster soup?

HIM. Yes I was afraid to tell you since you are paying.

HER. I'm glad you did choose it and glad that you are beginning to like it here That noisy gang in that private room over there seem also to like it, I think they are Masons or something.

HIM. Yes, quite possibly they are. You know, as soon as I got home this evening I knew that we were going out and not eating at home.

HER. How did you know?

HIM. Because there was no smell of burning.

HER. It's a good job these mushrooms are so nice and they cost so much or you would get them right between the eyes. You are an ungrateful b . . . . d. Do you know what day it is?

HIM. Wednesday, why?

HER. It is our twenty-fifth wedding anniversary, not that you would remember.

HIM. Oh sh . . . ! Did I forget it?

HER. Yes you have.

Later when eating was over > > > > > > >

HIM. Well it was nice of you to remember, even though I didn't, and the meal was great. The steak was fantastic, I thought 'Señor Straccaciatella' would cook it himself at the table, but in fact I cooked it myself on that red hot stone. When it arrived I thought it was raw, but it cooked itself on the stone. And what about you knocking back that load of cream on your Pineapple Romanoff, after you made a pig of yourself with that Tornados Rossini on 'pâté de fóe gras.' What will they say at your fatties club when you tell them that you had a ton of fresh cream?"

HER.   I won't tell them, because I would have to tell them why we went out and that you forgot.

HIM.   Well, I'm sorry. Why don't you order some coffee and if you dare, ask for the bill. You did say you were paying.

HER.   Waiter could we have some coffee. And then may we have the bill please.

>>>>>>> *Waiter arrives with coffee etc.* >>>>>>>>>>>>>

WAITER.   Your Coffee Madam and your bill, Sir?

HIM.   "Thank you. Pass it to Madam she will deal with it."

After scrutiny of the bill by her. > > > > > > > >

HER.   I think there is something wrong with this bill. It is only £14.36."

HIM.   Let me see.

HER.   Here look.

HIM.   So it is, it's too much wrong to just pay it and get out before they notice. You will have to be a good girl and play the honest. Call 'Señor Straccaciatella' and tell him.

HER.   I suppose so. Catch his eye for me.

HER.   Waiter I think there is an error on the bill. You have only charged £14.36.

WAITER.   "No mistake, Sir, Madam, £14.36 is correct. I hope you have enjoyed you meal"

HER.   It was very nice, thank you, but how can it be correct?

WAITER.   It is correct Madam. Two days ago this gentleman kindly came into the restaurant and paid £50 in advance Madam. He explained everything and, may I congratulate you both on attaining your 25th anniversary. Will that be all Madam? Enjoy your coffee and could I offer you both a liqueur on the house since it is your very special occasion?"

HIM.   Well that would be very nice for me, thank you, I would accept a Grand Marnier but madam has exceeded her calorie ration.

HER.   Yes, thank you; it's very kind of you. I will have a Cointreau."

WAITER.   Very well Madam.

While enjoying their liquors > > > > > >

HER.   How did you come to pay in advance?"

HIM.   Ah well, it's a long story. The other day, when you were spending all the housekeeping on a hair-do for some frippery occasion or other, like our wedding anniversary, did you think I didn't know what day the hair-do was for? The maitré d rang to say that he would be very much obliged if we could change the time of our meal to 7.0PM He explained that he had a large party booked for the evening and he didn't want us to be inconvenienced by having to wait for them to be served. I realised that you were planning some sort of surprise and beat you to it. It was a great meal, thank you for asking me, and the, company, it is the best in the world, although I say it myself, it is 'par excellence', but I still think this place is expensive.

HER.   For the occasion it was not expensive. I was keeping it from you, but I got four numbers on the lottery and won £117, I decided to spend, spend, and spend on a good night out. As you have paid in advance why don't we order bottle of something and stay for a while? It will be difficult but I think that I could endure your company here for a bit longer.

Later still when the bottle is empty > > > > > > > >

HIM.   Now you might think that I am getting drunk but I also had some excellent good fortune and I won in a lottery. My win was of far greater value than your measly £117 pounds.

HER.   You never told me about it.

HIM.   No, not in so many words but you knew of it.

HER.   What did I know and what did you win?

HIM.   Oh! It was some twenty five years ago.

HER.   Well what did you win?

HIM.   I won you.

*   *   *

WHAT ABOUT A HIAKU NOW

Sunbeams through the leaves.
All colours of the rainbow
Dancing in the wind

For years Mr Buttlar had been visiting Mrs Cartwright's guest house, spending three or four days at a time in the off season. He always occupied what she said was one of her 'standard' rooms. Standard was a euphemism for inferior, but her cooking and the portions thereof were ample compensation. She seldom had other guests when he was there, a travelling salesman, or perhaps a senior citizen couple, more often ladies in retirement.

This morning quite a different type of guest came to take breakfast. Mr Buttlar was seated at a table and, having finished his cereal and juice, he awaited Mrs Cartwright to bring his regular toast and full English breakfast. In she came with her tray on which was a double-egg, full, English breakfast.

"Good morning Mr Buttlar. I hope you slept well."

"Yes, very well thank you Mrs Cartwright." He never made more conversation than was barely necessary to maintain politeness.

"We have another guest today." she said joyfully, no doubt thinking of the extra revenue. "Captain Newson, a retired headmaster from Liverpool, but he must also have been a military man. He has taken one of my superior rooms. Oh, here he is. Good morning Captain, I hope you slept well? This is Mr Buttlar, one of my regular guests. Mr Buttlar, this is Captain Newson."

"Yes, thank you madam," said a positive Captain Newson, "it is a very comfortable bed and there is an excellent pastoral view from the window. Do I help myself to the cereals? "And turning to Mr Buttlar, "Good morning Mr Buttlar, and how do you do?" He offered his hand, but Mr Buttlar just held his knife near his mouth in a gesture of acknowledgment and signalling that his mouth was full.

"Yes, help yourself to the cereals and what would you like to follow? One of my full English breakfasts?" she said as she began to lay the cutlery on the table opposite Mr Buttlar. "I'll put you on the table with Mr Buttlar, and then you can both get acquainted."

Mr Buttlar did not speak, but surreptitiously moved the toast rack nearer to his plate.

"Yes," said the Captain, "but not two of everything, one egg etc will be sufficient, and tea, thank you," as he sat down with his cereal, opposite Mr. Buttlar.

"I always eat a hearty breakfast and then go for a good stiff walk. Keeps you fit you know." The Captain made an involuntary stretch of his neck and shake of his head as he made the statement. "I used to tell my pupils, 'Have a good breakfast and do some exercise each morning, such as run to school.'" In all his years of teaching in Liverpool it had never occurred to him that many of his pupils may not have had even a slice of toast before leaving home to do his suggested run. "How do you spend your days here Mr Buttlar?"

Mr Buttlar was about to answer, but was glad when Mrs Cartwright entered with the Captain's egg and bacon.

She set the food down saying, "There you are! You enjoy that. And here's the Telegraph that you ordered." She cleared the cereal dishes and placed the newspaper in the now-free space, with the front page and headline on view.

"Thank you Mrs Cartwright," said the Captain, "And what do you do when you are not here Mr Buttlar?"

"What?" said Mr Buttlar as he for the first time raised his eyes from his plate?

"Yes, what do you do for a living," asked the Captain

"Piano tuner."

"I never knew that Mr Buttlar," said Mrs Cartwright who had lingered to earwig on the conversation.

"A piano tuner? I sidelined music for the pupils at my school. Oh yes, they made a noise at morning assembly, but music was something with which they would never cope. Standing atop of the dustbin cart would be the pinnacle of any career rise that any of them might make."

Mr Buttlar did not make any comment to either.

The Captain seemed to ask questions, but not wait to receive or follow up on any answers, as though he was not interested in the replies. Looking at the headlines he commented, "It looks as if Germany is to have its first woman Chancellor."

Mrs Cartwright broke in, "Don't they have women Councillors in Germany? There are six on our council." "Chancellors, Mrs Cartwright," said the Captain, with distain in his voice, "are like Prime Ministers; Hitler was a Chancellor. I'll bet she's a daughter of that She-Devil, Irma Grese. The one who kept the keys at Buchenwald."

"Oh I've heard of her," said Mrs Cartwright, "she was wicked.

They do say she made lamp shades from the skin of tattooed prisoners."

"Yes my dear," The Captain was now talking as if to a boy who had done some good work, "She was wicked, they still are, those Germans."

Mr Buttlar did not comment, but took his fifth piece of toast and carried on eating his breakfast.

"What do you think Mr Buttlar, Germans are all black-hearted swine? That is what I used to tell the boy cadets that I commanded in 1940. Germans are all black-hearted swine. I was supposed to teach those boys English, but in the war it was imperative to teach them about those evil Germans."

Mr Buttlar was cornered. He had to reply and quietly said, "I would not say they are all like that."

"You know something about Germans do you? If you had been with me in 1916 you would have seen some of it first hand."

Mr Buttlar, not wanting to disagree, offered, "They say they bayoneted babies in the first war. Did you witness any of that?"

"Well not exactly that, but they did commit other atrocities," countered the Captain.

"That's it," said Mr Buttlar. "I never met anyone who actually saw those deeds in 1914, and when there were some reported in 1940, nobody believed the stories to be true."

"I can assure you that it was true. All true!" the Captain was now using his assertive voice.

Mrs Cartwright added, "Yes it was."

"Yes, those stories were true!" said the Captain, glad of the collaboration, "If you have never heard them, where did you spend the war, man?"

Again Mr Buttlar was obliged to make a reply, "Most of it, I spent not 100 meters from here."

The Captain burst with indignation, "You must have had a cushy number, stationed here away from the bombs and fighting."

"Before that I was in Heidelberg," Mr Buttlar said quietly, as he reached for the marmalade.

"What were you doing there?" The Captain had deflated a little.

"I lived there, and when I was brought to England I was brought here to this town."

"You are a German then, and were a prisoner of war? We should have shot you! Not brought you here. I always said, 'Take no prisoners'," said the Captain, bursting with pomposity.

Mr Buttlar was obviously uncomfortable in the presence of this self-opinionated man but continued. "When I first came to this town I was taught English by some eminent professors of the subject and I sometimes played the piano to entertain the forces."

"You learnt English in this country?"

"Exceptionally well, in better times we would all have qualified for a MA. in the subject." Mr Buttlar avoided the full truth, "There were 43 of us billeted up the road. We learnt English and eventually became spies of a kind. Actually Robert Maxwell was one of us. We were so good at English grammar that most of us went into the printing world after the war."

The Captain jumped to another conclusion, "Maxwell was not a prisoner of war, and he escaped to England!"

"So did I," said Mr Buttlar after taking his time to finish his cup of tea.

"So you escaped from the Germans and avoided the swines and a concentration camp and you don't agree that they are all wicked?" implored the Captain.

"No," Mr Buttlar quietly replied, "there were some good Germans."

"You amaze me," said the Captain pulling himself to up and leaning towards Mr Buttlar, "I still say the only good Germans are dead ones. Anyway, you say you learnt English here? Where were you born? What is your mother tongue?"

"Leipzig and German," Mr Buttlar said, as he tackled yet another piece of toast. "My father was the resident conductor of the orchestra in Heidelberg. He was a German, but not a 'Black-Hearted Swine.' If you were a teacher of English you will know that 'ALL,' in English grammar is a determiner. That is, a modifying word that determines the kind of reference a noun or noun group has, for example a, the, every, the greatest possible, the total extent of, and 'all'. I, would choose the determiner 'some'. That is some of the Germans were and some still are, 'Black-Hearted Swine.' Now, if you were to say that some Englishmen are **'Unhöfliche Schweine'** then I would agree with you."

Ignorant swine

SILLY SIMILES FOR BIGGER CHILDREN

I'm as happy as a worm, with a body that's amphistomus,
I'm as happy as a bumblebee, with honey quite mellifluous.
I'm as lonely as a hyena, with its pusillanimous streak.
I'm as happy as a sandpiper, with acuminated beak.

I'm as happy as a hippo, with a bird for symbiosis,
I'm as sad as any Heart would be, with coronary thrombosis.
I'm as unhappy as an elephant, that's got a nasty cold.
I'm as unhappy as a walrus, when it's getting rather cold.

I'm as sad as a centipede, with its expensive pedicure.
I'm as happy as a parasite, whose life's a sinecure.
I'm as happy as a song-thrush, with cadence in its voice.
I'm as sad as an old pack mule, with nothing to rejoice.

I'm as lonely as a skunk, is with its odour most egregious.
I'm as happy as a slippery eel, whose skin is oleaginous.
I'm as happy as a snake that can excoriate his skin.
I'm as happy as a sly old fox, with a chicken at his chin.

I'm as happy as a lugworm that never gets fibrosis,
I'm as sad as every dragon with their awful halitosis.
I'm as happy as a cobra with its fissilingual tongue.
I'm as happy as marsupials with pockets for their young.

I'm as sad as a stick-insect, when he sniffs insecticide.
I'm as happy as a bull-frog, with an insect in its inside.
I'm as happy as a polar bear that never gets frostbite.
Or as happy as a hedgehog, with nocturnal appetite.

I'm as happy as a squirrel that plays at philopena,
I'm as lonely as ulcers are in peoples duodena.
Pity the spotted Cheetah who is sure he's been misnamed,
But in the world of taxonomy he is very well acclaimed.

It was a bright sun-shining morning. The beach was, at half past eleven, already filling with a tide of happy families, all carrying the accoutrements of the holiday maker, all rushing to stake their claims as if it were a Kansas land grab. The real tide, with its white topped waves was far out in the distance beyond a shimmering expanse of sand.

"Let's stay up here; I feel like a cup of tea; shall we sit here on this veranda?"

"You always want tea. I would rather have an ice cream, but yes, it may be a good idea to grab a seat in the shade."

"You are so right; it will be a good idea. Right, then, off I go one tea and one Cornetto. Don't go away; it may take until tomorrow, just look at the queue."

Well, I'm in the queue; it won't take until tomorrow. Look at this proportionally challenged guy in front. The last time I saw a rear end like that it was in the Serengeti National Park. Why does he need to bring his two deck chairs, which will never bear his weight, with him in a queue for ice cream?

"Fine day isn't it mate?"

Be polite now, talk to him, "Yes it is, but I don't think it will last the day out."

"You've been listening to those lying weather forecasters. They said that all hell would be let loose today. Lying sods, just look at it. The sun is cracking the 'sand'. I grabbed these deck chairs just in time. There are no more at this end of the beach and none at the other end either."

"You are very lucky, but I think I'll stay and sit on this veranda. No-one else seems so inclined."

"Don't you mean there is no more room on the beach?"

"I'll bet there will be plenty of room there later."

"You wouldn't win that bet mate, unless you mean when it goes dark. Look at this lot, thousands of them. They're going to soak up all of this sunshine."

"Hi dear, it's me at last, with one Cornetto and one tea. There was no chance that you would get fed up waiting. Now that you have your head in that book we're settled for the day."

"*Tempus fugit!* You have read about fifty pages and it is half past one. What about going inside for some proper food?"

"That steak was good, you wouldn't think that a, 'Greasy Spoon' joint like this could have such cuisine. And just listen to the gulls squawking. I know there will be lots of food about, but that noise means, 'When the gulls make for the shore it is going to rain'."

"Yes dear, I've heard that before."

"The tide is coming in fast now, driving those near the water to crowd into the few remaining spaces."

"Yes Dear," she said without raising her eyes from the book.

"If you can spare a second from your book, look over there beyond the lighthouse. See that bit of cloud forming?

"Yes Dear."

"I'll order more tea just to retain these seats. Would you like some?

"Yes Dear."

"Ah! That tea is good. Do you see that cloud like a long tongue? They call it an 'Anvil Cloud'. It also portends bad weather".

"Yes Dear."

"Here comes the wind. Look at the papers flying about! There will be lots of sand in the butties, but it is great for those kids with their kites. And look at those boats in the harbour. They look as if they are jostling for position."

"Yes Dear."

"There's a flash of lightning! While you have had your head in that book the cloud has grown and is now beginning to shed its load."

"Yes, dear, is it?"

There was a mad scramble on the beach. Mothers were calling and rounding up their broods who, were loath to abandon their sand artistry. They gathered their towels and clothes into bundles and were fleeing to the shelter of the arcades and cafes.

Mothers struggled to dress their off-spring with their now wet clothes, all pushing and shoving in the crowds on to the veranda where we had first sat. The wind was blowing so hard that all who now were inclined to seek shelter were, in fact, 'inclined' against the wind pressure.

It was now raining with such violence that one could not see the lighthouse but the light still gave off its regular intermittent glow. A sudden flash seemed to strike the light and a simultaneous, tremendous bang shook the building. Children, now feared, began to cry. Stressed mums' and dads' voices grew to crescendo. The boats in the harbour which were apparitions and barely visible, were smashing their masts and yard-arms together as if in a courtship routine. They pitched and rolled in a frantic sea which had been a placid harbour not three hours earlier. The canvas awning of the adjacent café was ripped apart and now two large red and white striped flags lashed at everything and everybody within their compass. There was also a deluge of spray sweeping onto our veranda, such that all who wished shelter were as wet as if they had been swimming. Every-one, mums, dads and children were frantically appealing vainly to each other for assistance.

Another bolt of lightning and thunder struck something along the promenade which could not have been more that two hundred yards away. The noise was deafening. It raised a simultaneous chorus of, 'Wooah!' from all throats and several large pieces of plastic roofing cantered along the prom from that direction.

The tide reached its high mark long before its appointed time. Deck chairs galore and some spades were now heaps of flotsam, embedded in a heap of jettisoned paper cups, plastic bottles and other detritus. The odd abandoned bucket rolled up and down the remaining strip of sand.

We were sitting comfortably within the protection of the glass windows of this café when, who should push his way in, but the large dad. He was obviously a dad as he trailed five children behind him and was followed by an equally pushy wife. with two others.

"See you chose right," he said, as he gathered the five to him and instructed his wife to push and get some victuals, if only as an excuse to shelter in the café.

"Yes I would have won the bet."

"Yes you win, turned out nice weather for fish hasn't it?"

"Yes it has turned out very nice for me."

"You mean that you really had a bet on the weather?"

"To be sure I did, didn't I Dear?"

"Yes Dear."

"How could you be so sure as to bet on it?"

"I may not look like one, but I am actually a Fish, aren't I Dear?"

"Yes Dear."

"I'm Michael Haddock. I do the weather forecast, don't I Dear?"

"Yes Dear."

*   *   *

Written 8 March 2012

THE LAST WAR

It was the war to end all wars, that is what they said.
But that was only practice for another one ahead.
Those soldiers fought for freedom and true democracy,
A land that's fit for heroes would be the legacy.
But those who hold the power, captains of industry,
Never really meant it, for the likes of you and me.

We believed all this, it was simply idiotic
No matter how hard one tried, the task was asymptotic.
With insufficient work about, stomachs went unfilled,
The populace discovered that they had all been shilled,
Hope which springs eternally, was very nearly killed,
And all those promises of the past went mostly unfulfilled.

Another crop of heroes were not yet fully grown,
Before the dogs of war had sniffed, the alluring pheromone.
Land was grabbed by nations, to enlarge their pitch,
Franchises and contracts were garnered by the rich,
Mineral recourses were annexed without a hitch,
While members of a great cabal decide on who gets which.

We have had wars by the dozens in perpetuity.
And folk have borne their burden with equanimity.
A war to end all wars they said, but had them hot and cold,
Today we hear of Heroes, brave and also bold,
Six callow youths, whose lives were greatly undersold,
But all is well they say, their families have been told.

*   *   *

The bus was running late again. It was now forty minutes late. Mary was not aware that it ever ran late but she had just gleaned this information from the conversation of two ladies sitting behind her on the long distance bus.

"Joe will be waiting for us; he will be missing his pint and not too delighted."

"The pubs will be shut and the place will be deserted when we get in."

Hearing this, Mary became anxious. She had intended to get the last bus to the university. That bus would have long gone. She would be in a relatively strange town, very late at night.

The ladies began to collect their belongings, indicating to Mary that they were close to journey's end. The bus pulled into the terminus and the three passengers alighted. The driver extracted their luggage from the luggage compartment and, before Mary could gather her thoughts, the bus had sped off. A car which had awaited the ladies sped off with them. Standing in the darkness, she could just make out the forms of two cars parked at the side of the ticket office.

Mary walked to the main road thinking that she might get a lift to the university. She noted the name of the road, or rather two names. To the left was Country Road North and to the right was Country Road South. Which? She thought. This was where she ought to apply her non-existent, hitch-hiking talent.

Anxiously looking about her, Mary noticed a torch light flicker near the station office. She went back to the office and could see that there were two men and they were preparing to leave. One was locking up and, when the other had seen his partner fasten the last lock he said, "Goodnight Dusty," and went off to one of the cars.

Mary had only this 'Dusty' from whom she could request help. She asked which direction she ought to go on the Country Road to reach the University Halls of Residence.

"Take the North Road to the University." said Dusty, but he was intrigued, and asked, "You are going to walk with those two bags all the way to the Uni Halls?"

Mary said sheepishly, "I was hoping to hitch a lift, perhaps a student with 'wheels' might come by."

"But it's no place for a girl on her own at this time of night. If you don't lose those two bags, you will most probably lose something much more important. Where did you say you were going?"

"To the University Halls of Residence," she confided.

"I go past there, I would gladly give you a lift, but it's not wise for you to accept lifts from strangers." He sounded very serious.

"What can I do?" she implored, "I'm at risk if I try hitching a lift, and I'm at risk if I accept a lift?"

"I'll tell you what you do," he said with a decisive tone, "have you got a mobile?"

"Yes." Mary confided.

"Well," he said, "You ring your parents and tell them that you are just about to get a lift in Dusty's, the cashier's car, registration JF04 BHD and to check you are still safe in thirty minutes." Then he picked up her bags and walked to his car while she fumbled in the dark with the phone.

He sat in his car waiting while she did as instructed. Once in the car Mary relaxed.

"Obviously you are a student. Where have you come from, and what is your name?"

"A long way, from Newcastle, two changes of bus and fifty minutes late." Mary answered. "My name is Mary Miller, I've been home for the first time,' but I don't think I will bus it home again."

"A Geordie," he mused. "I only know two things about Newcastle: Shipbuilding and the Blaydon Races. Do you come from a family of jockeys then?"

"No, not that prestigious, Dad was in shipbuilding, but he gave my Mum a rough time and she left him, or he left her."

There was a long silence, and then he asked, "What are you reading?"

"I hope to be a journalist," enthused Mary.

"A journalist," said Dusty, "On something a bit better than the Northern Echo I hope, got your sights on the New York Times have you?" and then, "Here we are, you are safe up to now. I'll wait until you are inside and making that call."

He took the bags from the boot and hesitated thoughtfully before he said. "I am on duty every week-end. If you go home again let me know and I will look for you. Put my number in your phone for emergencies." Then he wrote it on the luggage label of her grip.

Weeks later Mary received a letter at the Halls, it contained two theatre tickets. They had been sent by Dusty, with a note which read, 'I am involved with an amateur dramatic group and it is incumbent upon me to purchase some tickets. I thought you and one of your friends might like to use them. It is a two-act play, 'The Law Is A Hass.' If you miss the last bus I will see you safely to the halls.'

On the night, Dusty was pleased to see Mary and a friend, another hopeful journalist, Polly Propylene in the audience.

At the interval Dusty was keen to know what the budding theatre critics thought of it so far.

"It's a bit like Kramer versus Kramer, with more antagonism, especially from the mother," Mary ventured.

Her friend, Polly, added, "The mother is portrayed as a right bitch; the Social Services woman seems very gullible, 'two pence short of a shilling', and the judge seems as though he is picking winners and not taking notes. Is that what is intended? Don't tell us who gets custody of the child, but from where did the author get the strange spelling in the title?"

"Oh, I think that it came from Dickens, via Mr Bumble," Dusty offered.

Pleased at their interest, he assured them that there would be many twists in the final courtroom act."

All went well with the performance. The exit poll gave 'highly recommend' plaudits. So did the two critics. Dusty asked the girls to be patient while he did a few chores, but almost instantly he was neglecting his duties and was more interested in the girls' opinions.

Mary, too, had much to contribute, "I was disappointed with the ending," she said, "I expected the father to get custody, but there was no way the authorities were going to believe the father."

Polly commented, "It was clever how the author made the mother's word so plausible, and the actress played it well, she made you believe her word about ill-treatment of the child, while all the time she was coveting the family home for herself and her lover."

A lady actress added to the discussion, "What about the mother's claim that he had not provided financial support for child?"

"That puzzled me," interrupted Polly, "Is that the way courts proceed in such cases? They refused to accept almost any evidence as though their minds are made up. Sort of, 'don't confuse us with evidence.' Even though there were ages of bank statement evidence of her receiving money."

"Perhaps that is where the title springs from," said Dusty.

All agreed, though the outcome was not altogether a happy one, it was a good play.

On the way back to the halls Mary pondered aloud, "I wonder if my Mum and Dad had a set to like that?" then added, "By the way we are thinking of going home this week end, Polly to Leeds and me to Newcastle. Can we take your offer of a taxi and your protection?"

"Of course, anytime."

On Sunday night, the bus was again late. The girls were full of appreciation for Dusty's help.

The following Sunday, Mary and Polly visited the bus station. "Hello Fairy Godfather," she said, poking her mobile through the hatch and taking his picture.

Dusty left his post for a while to be sociable and Polly greeted him saying, "Hi! Mary is showing off her new phone."

There was some chit-chat about where to eat and what to see and Dusty returned to his hatch.

On the following Sunday the girls paid Dusty another visit. This time he took his break. Over tea in a café, Mary said, "I sent the photo of our Fairy Godfather to my Mum. She rang me; she seemed flustered, saying she knew you and you haven't changed."

"Isn't that a coincidence," exclaimed Dusty.

"What is your real name?" Mary questioned.

"George Miller, Miller like yours. All Millers are called Dusty. It is a wonder that you weren't called the same"

Polly intervened, "We looked at the programme for the play and the author's name was George Miller."

"Another coincidence?" said George with a smile.

"Mum said she is sure you are my dad, could that be so?"

"Yes, that is a possibility," replied Dusty.

"Are you sure? Mary queried, "You don't seem to be like Mum has portrayed you all these years."

"That night when you said your name was Miller and I wrote my phone number on your luggage label, I read and noted your address. I knew then who you were and could not believe my luck."

Polly interrupted. "Was your play based on true life?"

Dusty looked at Mary, and with a nod that indicated yes, said, "I'm afraid it was, almost every word of it."

"Even to saving all the bank statements?" Mary asked.

"And years of the mortgage repayments," added Dusty.

"Mum never had a good word to say about you. She always claimed that you beat me but I can't remember anything like that. In fact I can't remember anything about you. I must have been very young. Mum always said that you never wanted to see me, and yet after you left, you subsidised us for all those years?"

"And that bloke she lives with, he has been living in my house for fifteen years. I subsidised him too," Dusty said, with a touch of malice. "But it will soon change."

Mary didn't understand this.

"Be here next week at the same time and I will explain all. But now I must get back to the station."

When the next Sunday arrived, Mary and Polly were waiting in the café. Dusty had a holdall containing teddies and other cuddly toys, which he was forced to drop when Mary threw her arms around his neck and hung on tightly saying, amid sobs, "You are my Dad, you are my Dad." And he hung on to her just as tightly, unable to hold back his tears.

Mary had spoken with her mother who had no alternative but admit to the payments and reluctantly, to her vindictiveness.

Polly watched and waited patiently until Mary relaxed her hold and they sat down.

Dusty did all the talking while Mary and Polly listened. He opened the holdall saying, "Here are the toys that I tried to give you but your mother would not let me near you. She had to keep up the lie that I mistreated you. I would not let her get the equity in the house so I kept it and allowed you to live in it rent-free. I paid the mortgage because if I stopped, though I wasn't bothered about her, you would have had to live in an inferior neighbourhood. I loved you too much to allow that." He handed her his handkerchief, "In eighteen months time, you will be twenty. The house, my house, will be yours. I paid the mortgage for you, not her. You can sell it over her head if you wish, but as you have some of my genes I don't think you will be that malicious."

There was so much hugging that a red-eyed Dusty was late, but ever so light-hearted returning to his ticket office.

NONSENSE POEM

In the place called Nagasaki,
Which is north of Sarawaki.
Lived a bloke who smoked tobbaki,
Which has sent him rather wacky.

He bought the wacky backy,
In a shacky called the snacky,.
From a lackey who was tacky,
Who they all called Allie Smacky.

This lackie, Allie Smacky,
Sold a lot of wacky baccy.
To the man from Nagasaki,
Who in time became quite yaky.

His brain became a jelly,
And it wobbles like his belly.
His clothes are rather smelly,
Like that of an old wellie.

He now sits watching Tele,
Even watches Telewele.
Or looking nonchalantly,
At the button of his belly.

In fact he's actually,
Non compos mentis-ally.
In a torpor medically,
And straight jacket physically.

Unless you're doodlally,
With that baccy never tally.
Or you'll be tragically,
Non-Grata Personally.

WHAT POEM

For homework write a poem,
That's what the teacher said.
Rhyming? No, not one of those,
A haiku instead.

There is no need to make it rhyme,
It matters not a jot.
Just count the bits on every line,
She'll like it quite a lot.

She told us to take note of rhyme,
Whenever it occurred.
I note that frost is made of rime,
And cold although it's furred.

Shall I make it Elegiac?
And copy that guy Gray.
She'll think me paranoiac,
I'll write it anyway.

No don't do that, it's just a whim,
Try a standard stanza.
I surely will impress her,
With my great extravaganza.

If I try pentameters.
With verse of just five feet.
Or even hexameters,
She'll think that rather neat.

Whatever style I write in,
Dactyl-Tanka-Doggerel.
It shows that I'm no cretin,
With that she cannot quarrel.

To Sir John Cholmondeley Bt.
Isandhlwana
30 August 1884

Dear Chummers,

At last I can report some good hunting. We have driven a track through the pass, the work on which was delayed by the onset of rain, as I described in my last communication. As yet it is suitable only for mules or pack animals. This done, we sought to benefit and took the advantage to reconnoitre the hinterland beyond and seek out any game, not for sport exactly but more for 'the pot.' So, leaving the boys to widen the track and create a section of a road over land that has never been disturbed since God created it, we made ready for a ten week safari. This, we had estimated, would be enough for them to complete

the task, or at least, not require our guidance. We detached twenty good strong boys to carry our victuals, ordnance, tenting etc and left Creighton to oversee the workings; Urquhart, Martineau, Fortescue and I then set off in good spirits, having been assured by the 'savvy' boy that we would find big and good hunting in the region, near the village of Ginghilovo, which is the eventual terminus of our construction project.

Having made good progress for five days we came across a meandering river which, considering the recent rain was far from full flood. In some parts it was no more than a Mangrove swamp. In others there were large expanses of black, ankle deep, evil smelling; stomach wrenching, mud, in which armies of crawling and slithering, smelly creatures wallowed. Here we sighted some Water Buffalo and the occasional Hippo. Fortescue bagged himself a gazelle, which, when

prepared, made a tasty viand. The meanders were of such dimension that we were forced to cross the river several times to avoid miles, or perhaps days, of detour. At each of these crossings we were carried by the boys, sturdy chaps, who conveyed us over and through the swamps. One of the boys, while crossing the river, carrying a large box of dash (Baksheesh for the natives in your Raj days) went out of line and found himself floundering in deeper water. He was stuck in the mire, as if he were rooted to it. The blighter would have discarded the goods; it was in fact two bales of cloth, some string and some beads; had I not threatened him with my pistol. He soon came to his senses and moved from his stubborn position and found extra strength in his feet and legs.

Little did we know of the dangers and terrible fate that might have engulfed us! But I will tell of this later.

Four further days had passed in the region of the river, after which we were again on *terra firma*. Then followed six more days of relatively flat terrain; stopping for six hours on one of the days, whilst a large herd of Zebra crossed our path. There is no sport in taking from a herd but the boys are partial to Zebra so Fortescue took one out for them. We then came upon a, narrow track through the thick African bush. This we followed for a further two days.

I must here remind you that the route over which we were

travelling is probably the same as the Zulus travelled some years ago, after they had overwhelmed and slaughtered the 1700 men of Lord Chelmsford's force at Isandhlwana. You will recall that the Zulus then moved on to Rorke's Drift, where they were given a bloody nose by some 120 chaps of the Welsh Regiment.

To continue, we followed this path until we blundered upon a small native kraal. Although we had only a fleeting sight of natives, we could hear the frightened shrieks from the local fauna as the humans ran in fear from us. We eventually caught a woman carrying her baby and held her. She fought and struggled to free herself but on showing and giving her some beads, she calmed down and she guided us to a kraal and to the headman. It was only a single household. He was not a chief and this was not Ginghilovo.

This man, might have been Methuselah, for he had more lines on his face than Brunel's railway. He drove a hard bargain for 'dash,' before he condescended to show us where, he said, we could find game and the village of Ginghilovo. Even then we placed little confidence on his ability to tell the truth. For two days we travelled through miles of thick, slushy, muddy, swamp, for we had encountered the river again. We, as I have said, were carried on the shoulders of the natives or in their canoes when crossing the river. All this time we had not a single sight of game of any type. Eventually on the third day we arrived at a large group of kraals. The natives here came out to greet us. This, we discovered was in fact the village of Ginghilovo, where the chief, who was seemingly of some importance in the district, entertained us right royally. It was here that we were told that crocodiles abound in these parts. We doubted the veracity of such claims. Our doubts were heightened by the fact that we had been wallowing in the mangroves for near three weeks and had not seen or been aware of such danger as was described by this chief. He told of one great crocodile that was lately killed and in its stomach there were found two human sculls and many bones. He said crocodile was very, very, hard to find and kill as they usually hid from sight and when sighted almost always manages to slink away out of sight.

Such monsters as this chief described indeed whetted our appetite. If, indeed, the beasts were as large as the chief had described, that being some 30 feet in length, we could not wait to try our hand at such game. In evidence of such creatures we were shown crocodile artefacts, teeth skins and the like. There was however still nagging doubt as to whether such large specimens did exist, for we had not seen any sign of a crocodile, big or small, on our journey.

Taking our goods and chattels with the intention of being in the bush for some time, there then followed a near full-day trek back into swamp, to where we expected to encounter the big man-eaters.

We were accompanied by half the village population, following on at a discreet distance. Knowing that we were after game they hoped to get some portion of the kills for their pots. We were brought to a large backwater pool of slow-flowing water, and assured that here we would find crocodile. With regard to size of our expected prey, had they been fly fishermen we would certainly have taken their gesticulations as exaggeration. But if we were to encounter such specimens we confirmed among ourselves that there would be no stories about, 'The one that got away.'

The four of us scoured the bank for a mile or two for evidence of crocodile but there was none. We waited and waited. It is tedious work waiting for a man-eater to come out of the water. I considered what we might use as a lure. Getting impatient, I grabbed a fat native child who had strayed too near to us. Of course its Mamma would and did object to its being pegged down as food for a great crocodile. Trying to make a bargain for the loan of the infant would be a time consuming negotiation and expensive in 'dash.' So there it was pegged down, and its mother, wailing like a banshee. It did not take long for, truly, a monster to come out of its lair. Viewing the tempting morsel tethered carefully to a bamboo at a well chosen distance from the waters edge, he made a rush through the reeds. Unfortunately for the brute he gave us warning of his approach when he disturbed the reeds.

My sportsmen friends, ready to fire, were hidden behind some reeds; they had given me first shot. It did not miss. My bullet penetrated its heart. The monster was dead in seconds.

The bait, who had been alarmed only by the firing, was returned to his mother none the worse for his experience. The mother, of course, was still remonstrating and to placate her we gave her first choice of the animal for her pot, along with some three yards of cloth. Of course we paid heed to protocol and let the headman have the real first choice. With her share she was much pleased and would have offered her offspring for further sport. Such was her confidence in our skill.

There were further crocodile kills, without using the bait but none as large. The beast was full 30 feet 8 inches long. Fortescue bagged one nearly equal, it being 29 feet one inch. On the whole it was much the better than shooting hippo or rhino or pig sticking.

The villagers, having much for their pots, made a great fuss of us. This will stand us in good stead when we progress the road up to their village. Exciting it certainly was.

Thank you for the copies of 'The Times', they are much appreciated. I shall not bother you with details of our construction progress. Creighton, good fellow, is a sterling chap for keeping our reports. He sends them regularly to the Society. You can keep up with them there.

Hope you and her Ladyship are keeping in good health. Give her my good wishes.

Ever yours

George Featherstone-Haugh.

FISHER WOMAN'S TALE

My husband loves his fishing,
In sea, lake or running stream.
Though the weather may be perishing,
He'll still sit there and dream.

I sometimes sit beside him,
When the sun decides to shine.
He would give a proverbial limb,
If a fish would bite his line.

Alone he gazes into space,
He never sees the flowers.
His hopes are set on a pan-sized plaice,
That someday will be ours.

I sometimes bring along a book,
He brings a box of maggots.
He baits the line and slings his hook,
Then we wait, a few more hours.

Fish are rising clear to see,
Whenever he baits his line.
It seems to happen constantly,
Time after time after time.

He really gets excited,
Like a child on its birthday.
But the truth is never invited,
Re, the one that got away.

Here or there or anywhere,
In any kind of weather.
The catch is neither here nor there,
So long as we're together.

* * *

The 2.15 train for Leicester had just pulled out and removed the milling crowd where now on their way to Leicester. Those left on the platform were widely dispersed. Coming down the stairs and striding along towards the coffee bar, was a tall, young, stiff soldier, in camouflage denim and a large pack on his back. Using two steps to one of his, was a trim lady, possibly in her Sunday best, all matching ensemble and appearing to have come straight from the hairdresser.

Entering the coffee bar which was also somewhat empty he made for a vacant table near the window. She puffing a bit sat down while he took off his pack.

Looking around to scan the wares on offer he said to her, "Sit her mum while I go to see the train times, I must have about half an hour." He then left her scrutinising the menu board.

Seeing that there were no customers at the counter she ventured to leave his kit and order for both of them returning quickly to her seat

He was soon striding back and a smile appeared on her face as if he had been away for weeks. As he sat down she said, "I have ordered coffee for you and tea for me, and I have ordered for you a toasted tea cake, you always had, 'Teestead Toecakes' when we went into a café. I don't suppose you get many tea cakes where you are going."

"Sometimes, when things are quiet we have niceties like that but not too often."

A waitress brought the coffee and tea cakes saying, "We don't usually give table service but who could resist a chance to chat up a hulk like him,"

He replied, "You have left it late girl, my train goes in twenty minutes"

"I'll leave you then but I'll be here when you get back," she said and then she left them to talk.

"There are not many of them, out there either," he said as he made a sideways shake of his head, "whether it's quiet or not."

With a bit of a tear mum said, "It is the not quiet times that I worry about when you are out there."

"Oh! Mum, don't be like that I will be back sure as hell I will, and we will meet here and see if we get a free coffee from that sassy one there."

Just then two soldiers passed the window and seeing him, gave him a thumbs up to which he acknowledged.

He said, "A couple of the lads heading for the bar,"

She very reluctantly said, "Do you want to go to them now?"

"No mum, I'll stay with you until the train comes, but when it does, will you stay in here and you won't fit in with all that macho stuff out there."

Reaching out to hold his hand she said, "I understand son, but this time will you let me give you a kiss before you go?

Giving her hand an encouraging squeeze he said, "It's a deal, you can give me a kiss. In here."

Almost immediately there was a kafuffle on the platform which indicated that the train was approaching. He stood up and so did she. She was still holding his hand. He reached down to grab the strap on his kitbag and the other went around her shoulder allowing her to give him the coveted kiss. To her surprise he gave her a kiss in return, a great big smacker on her cheek, hugging her at the same time.

He broke apart, then grabbed and hugged her for a second time saying "There now," and momentarily held her hand as he turned to leave the coffee bar.

She stood there looking out of the window and could see him with big laughs and camaraderie. As he put his foot on the train stair he looked towards her, waved with his hat and was gone.

She stood looking until the train pulled out and then sat down to dab her eyes with a handkerchief.

The waitress who had watched it all came to take the crocks away and asked, "Are you alright mum," with a big emphasis on the mum, "you sit here and I will get you another cup of tea."

She brought the tea and asked, "Where is he off to?"

"Thank you, do I owe anything, second time to Afghanistan," his Mum said in answering both questions.

"No," said the waitress, "the tea's on the house. I saw him, a guy like that who gives his mum a kiss and hugs like that; I've been looking for a feller like that. Do you fancy giving him my address?"

*   *   *

Dylan Thomas is the exponent of the Villanelle. This is my try.

WRITE NOT THEIR NAMES IN GOLD

Nations must find a better way than war.
We must not honour those who kill and maim.
Then all will live in peace for ever more.

Rapacious warmongers we should abhor.
Write not their names in gold in halls of fame.
Nations must find a better way than war.

Insist on truth from every aggressor.
No claiming that their wars are in God's name.
Then all will live in peace for ever more.

Arms dealing shall be made part of folklore.
To outlaw bombs must be the 'new clear' aim.
Nations must find a better way than war.

Then wailing wives and mothers will no more.
Have men returned in body bags or lame.
Then all will live in peace for ever more.

Jaw, jaw we know, is better than war, war,
A shibboleth all peoples must acclaim.
Nations must find a better way than war,
Then all will live in peace for ever more.

*   *   *

ANOTHER HIAKU

Seeds glide twirl and sail,
Find a niche in which to grow,
Sleep while there is snow.

Lucy Mainwaring's body clock was running fast. At the age of 32 she was not happy with the cards life had dealt her. She had not met her Prince Charming, (not that she was too fussy about the charming bit, but she did want a princely bank account with her catch.) A no-account Count would not do. Her life to-date had been as a 'Nine to five,' minor in the Civil Service, and all the time a dogsbody to her now-deceased parents. The residue of her parent's estate netted her £96,000. She had accepted a redundancy package of £20,000. Her accrued pension rights from the state and a private company would not pay out until she reached the age of sixty. With this meagre sum she had determined to find a Count with a big account.

She was in the Isle of Wight at the Cowes Regatta, staying at the Royal Hotel, the cost of which was eating into her nest-egg. She had come to Cowes during the Regatta, intending to mingle with the yachting fraternity in the hope of catching her big fish. However she was finding that 'gate-crashing' upper-crust parties was difficult. She had but two dresses suitable for such an occasion, and was wearing the best of them. That is, the best to show off her 36-26-38 shape. She lingered in the foyer, glass in hand, mingling among and blending with those who were awaiting the arrival of their friends.

To look the part she had to at least sip her expensive, Martini now and again, but it was difficult to make them last. The budget would not cover too many.

As hoped, in fact, better than she had hoped, Mr Right came by and made a pass. "Is it lively in there?" he asked.

"Yes," she lied, "I have come out for some air."

"In that case I think I'll sample some before I go in. Can I get you another drink?"

He was hooked.

Robert had a boat-repair yard and hired out boats and small yachts. He also ran what he said was a nice little earner of running executive trips/cruises or ferrying ex-pats to and from French and Spanish ports. He was also the son of Judge Lance Purbright.

This one might do, she thought. Although he was 50 years old, he seemed to possess the princely bit in reasonable measure, and there was the potential bonus of a judge's legacy. He certainly had the charming bit, and after exchanging CVs for a while Lucy (with her assets and parenthood exaggerated) told him she was intending to stay for the summer, but wanted a flat or somewhere a bit quieter than the Royal.

Robert, suitably impressed, suggested that they join the revellers.

"I suppose we had better make the grand entrance," she said, as she grabbed his arm and they both made towards the liveried doorman who was guarding the ballroom.

There was no trouble entering. It seemed that Robert was well known in town and, passing the time of day with the doorman, they entered without question.

Just by coincidence, so he said, Robert was running one of his executive trips over to France the next day.

Oh, she didn't have to subscribe. This was just as well, as she could not afford the fees he had described. Of course, she would love to come. She had nearly landed her fish on the first cast; all she needed now was a keep-net.

Several free trips followed, with Robert dancing attendance on her. She had taken a real fancy to him. He, in turn, was evidently besotted with her. He never made any inappropriate passes; strictly gentleman-like was he.

Robert found her a flat and she was sure she could hear wedding bells in the distance.

Lucy of course, had to keep her wits about her. She had to glean every bit of information she could. One way she could do this was to eavesdrop on the crew's talk, whenever she was invited aboard. Occasionally some of this talk did not quite fit the scene that Robert had painted and this perturbed her.

It seemed Robert was a womaniser, but he had not made a move on her. When he arrived at a port he sometimes disappeared on business, or so he said. Was he seeing another? And the crew often used 'Bob' to address him. Not, she thought a very formal way. As she understood it, on ships the protocol was always to address the master as 'Captain.'

However she hung on and wedding bells were definitely audible. Then one overhearing session she heard, "The owner is due this weekend, make sure we are ship-shape."

Who, she thought, was the owner? Although she tried to invite herself on that trip she was rebuffed. "Too many clients, full cargo," he joked.

Lucy determined to find out, was, from a distance, keeping a watchful eye on the passengers that Saturday. There were only three. One man not much older than Robert was getting a lot of attention. The other two seemed to be his lackeys. That trip, she noted, was very short of passengers.

Three days later when Robert returned the cosy evening was disturbed by the verbal battle that followed his claim and insistence that there was a full passenger list on the trip.

Cornered, he had to admit that it was not his craft but that he was crewing and running it for a city gent who was to remain anonymous. However, Robert was the owner of the boat-yard and his father, the judge, had for years kept him at a distance. This was because, in his father's words, "Some of your buying and selling ventures do not seem to have a legitimate buying element to them." They did meet now and then but he had been given to understand that there was nothing in the will for his 'delinquent' son.

Lucy taunted him with the ironical situation of he being the biter and she had planned to bite him.

The facile and charismatic Robert eventually soothed her temper and an amicable conversation followed. Robert, seeking to exploit any situation, suggested that if she really wanted to hit the jackpot he could surreptitiously introduce her to his father and all may not be lost. "You could, if you are up to it, marry the old sod; he can't last long. We could still keep the fire burning between us."

Lucy considered this offer and found it most attractive. She had a better and less expensive, chance of securing her goal. If it came to fruition and she had her jackpot, she could tell Robert to sling one of his hooks in his boat-yard.

Robert set about placating his father by going to London on some fictitious business and making it an excuse for one of their rare contacts. The offer of lunch was accepted with Robert having to submit to all manner of corrective instruction. To demonstrate to his father that his son had a legitimate occupation, he invited his father on a special four-day trip to the Normandy Beaches. This would include coach trips, stops for lunches, onshore accommodation and plenty of time and opportunity for Lucy to cast her net. After a lot of being far too busy father accepted, when it was 'coincidently' discovered that the only time his father had available for such leisurely indulgences was exactly the time of the trip.

Four days with Lucy, always placed within talking distance at tables and adjacent hotel rooms, how could an old widower repulse innocuous, amorous advances? She, in judicial language, had no fixed address, but was travelling, enjoying the fruits of her recently acquired and substantial legacy. In no time they were soon on first-name terms of Lance and Lucy.

He was a high court judge. As a conversational piece he told her that each October the Lord Chancellor summons all judges to the Palace of Westminster. Among other matters of state they were each given instructions as to what they will be doing for the coming year.

Lucy, not wishing to miss a chance, said, "I have never been inside the Houses of Parliament, will you all be wearing your robes and funny gaiters?"

"No not us, but the Lord Chancellor might be wearing his. There is usually coffee, sandwiches and the like. We are allowed to bring friends. If you would like to have a tour of the Houses of Commons and the Lords you must come with me. Come up to London for a few days. No need to book into a hotel, I have plenty of space for visitors. It would be all very proper. I have a housekeeper and a part time, 'Jeeves' as chaperons,' he assured her. "It will all be very decorous."

Things were moving very fast for Lucy. On reporting back to Robert he commented, "The old sod was far too busy to take time off, now he is finding all the time in the world to take a bit of skirt on a sightseeing tour of London. You must have impressed him."

Lucy considered the London visit a paramount success. She had rubbed shoulders with the really great, if not the really good, and had tasted the style of life to which she aspired.

She left Judge Purbright with a forwarding address of her supposed aunt, and it was less than a week before it was in use.

He had to go to Edinburgh, maybe for two weeks, to pontificate on some legal issue. Would she care to accompany him? He would give her the run down of Holyrood House, The new Parliament, and would give her a guided tour of Edinburgh Castle.

Of course she would. She had never been to Edinburgh; she would be delighted, and so was Robert who was all the time making sure to protect his interest.

From Edinburgh on the way back to London for another stay at his home, Lance confided as to how much he enjoyed her company and how kind it was of her to accompany such an old "lonely" fellow as himself.

Lucy picked up on the 'lonely' and squeezed every bit sympathy for him out of it. She feigned embarrassment at being with him in public. She had been out and about with him for the better part of two months. She had met a lot of his associates, and ventured to say that the decorum part was wearing thin. Nevertheless he begged her to stay at his London flat for a little longer.

After a few more of Lucy's feigned embarrassing moments she, 'reluctantly' agreed to his ardent request. She of course had no intention of doing otherwise.

She stayed for another week and when she raised the prospect of her leaving, Lance suggested that she make it a permanent stay with all the trimmings.

She again pretended to be surprised at his serious interest saying, "All your Noble Lords, and especially the Noble Ladies, would skit at you taking on a young dolly-bird like me. They would link you with the judge in Gilbert and Sullivan's Iolanthe who wanted to marry a fairy."

At which he replied, "There is an appropriate line or two in Iolanthe, 'Faint heart ne-er won fair lady'."

Lucy was thinking, "After I marry you, the quicker you get a faint heart the better." Not wishing to appear pushy she said that she wished to think about it for a few days. Then, three days later, she said that she would stay with her maiden aunt for a few days to see if 'the absence made the attraction grow fonder.' She was really intending to go to Robert to plan the next moves.

On the train from London, en route to Cowes, she read the headlines of a fellow passenger's newspaper. 'Judge Purbright's son meets with accident, in suspicious circumstances, police are not ruling out murder.' She panicked. The word murder caused her to reflect and worry. Who would murder? Why? And what motive?

She rushed to buy the paper at Weymouth and spent the boat trip mulling over the details. The police had obtained substantial evidence which would link Robert to a drug running cartel on the continent, and did not rule out a gang or contract killing. What should she do about Lance? Should she contact him to commiserate?

No, she was away with her aunt in the heart of country; she had not read the papers or heard the radio. 'Just sit it out for a week.'

The police had been doing their work searching both the boat yard and Robert's private apartment; his computer and his mail, and were interviewing associates etc.

The Inspector visited Lance to express his sympathies and ask, "A few questions." Inspector Halliwell produced some personal effects that had been Robert's saying that they had been recorded and if Lance would sign for them he could retain them.

Lance questioned why, as the effects seemed only to be several apparently personal letters addressed to Robert.

The Inspector was a bit uneasy saying, "I thought you might like to read them, especially the most recent one. You don't have to read them right now. It is unlikely that anything contained in them or any comment you might have about them will form part of any evidence. I don't, and I am sure you won't, want them to become exhibit, "Number umpteen," if we find there was foul play. I can assure you that only I and my assistant inspector have seen the contents and apart from you seeing them, that is how I would like it to stay."

Later, when the Inspector had left to go to interview Lucy, Lance opened and read the most recent letter as instructed.

Dear Robert,

The old bugger, as you call him, has fallen into our net. He wants an answer, 'Will I marry him?' He can't wait, and I have had him dangling for a few days and will leave him dangling a bit longer. I intend to return to you so that we can plan the next moves. How will I get into the will? Should I broach it before or after I say yes?'

Lance did not read any further, nor did he read any of the other letters. The Inspector's message was now very clear and he reflected, I must remember Inspector Halliwell and to thank him for his circumspection.

The inspector called on Lucy, considered that her misdeeds, though offensive, were not offences. Of course, if she had benefited from Robert's nefarious dealings that would be different. With this in mind he kept a watch on her standard of living and on her depleting bank balance. She had years to wait for her civil service pension and found herself employment in a post office as a counter-clerk and not a countess.

THE BIG IDEA

Cameron's got a big idea, but what's it all about,
He says a Big Society this fills me with some doubt.
I've asked a lot of people, there's nobody can say,
But while he's not expounding, the dole queue grew today.

To join the Big Society will membership be free?
If there's a cost incurred I don't think it's for me.
There's more than half of us scraping on basic pay,
Does he want us to be thankful? We're not, on the dole today.

Will it give us Tesco points or air miles to collect?
Until he tells us clearly he won't get much respect.
He wants us all to volunteer, we can only hope and pray,
That Dave really does know, the dole queue grew today.

Dave wants his lot of volunteers, Community minded folk,
Be trained to do some no pay jobs he says it's not a joke.
A chosen few will train us, and get fifty pound a day,
And another two thousand joined the queue today.

While Lib and Tory toadies applaud this absurdness?
He wants us all, to do much more, while they do so much less.
Us plebs make sacrificial cuts, while MPs make the hay,
Nobody, from Downing Street, joined the dole today.

There's fifty thousand pounds to spend, if you have a big idea.
The money comes from grannies bank, the one you didn't clear,
Three hundred million is lying there; he'll steal it that's OK,
And he does not give a monkey's about the dole today.

I'll volunteer for a surgeon, specialise in lobotomy,
We know he's lost his marbles, he could come to me.
I'd give him my best frontal, his fantasies to allay,
Then even he could volunteer, to join, the dole, today.

Father Kennedy has a dark secret with which he has lived for twenty years. He had diligently kept his vows and, apart from original sin, he considered himself to be pure in heart and soul. That was until his late thirties; he is now convinced that his soul is blacker than the hobs of hell.

His demise started twenty years ago to the day. That was the day his patron, the very rich Lady Marchbanks, died.

Father Kennedy, or Michael, was her father confessor, Priest of the local Holy Rosary Church, of which Lady Marchbanks was the chief benefactor. The church was, to all intent and purposes' an annex to Marchbanks Hall. The estate's journeymen attended to the maintenance of the Holy Rosary as if their instructions were outlined in a Papal Bull. The Bishop, with whom she was well acquainted, praised her for her generosity, but wished that she was as generous to the cathedral.

Father Kennedy was there that day, at her bedside, to see that she passed to the next world having made peace with her maker; being pure in heart and with a soul devoid of sin.

One month earlier they had both visited a preview of a forthcoming auction at Sotheby's. The one item on view was the very famous Madonna and child, sculpted by illustrious Antonio Bagarelei. The likely selling price of the piece was upwards of three quarters of a million pounds. Lady Marchbanks was besotted with it.

She confided to Michael that, as her husband had been the last in line of the Marchbanks and as they had no progeny, she had bequeathed the total of her considerable estate to the diocese and the Bishop. She then, at that late date wished to make a codicil and purchase the Madonna. He dutifully followed her instructions, getting some of her crested notepaper and a pen, and then, as she dictated he wrote:-

"I Lady Anne Marie Majoribanks of Marchbanks Hall, still being of sound mind, wish this codicil to be appended to my will which is held in the office of Edward Harvey and Co.

Notwithstanding anything heretofore written in the said will I instruct that sufficient finance be taken from my estate to purchase the Antonio Bagarelei.'Madonna and child.' Then it is to be placed on public exhibition in St Anne's Cathedral. Witness whereof, I have hereunder set my hand this day of Eighteenth October in the year of our Lord, One thousand nine hundred and sixty-two."

On the doctor's arrival, Michael was holding the unsigned document in his hand and, as the doctor was announced by her lady's maid, Michael greeted the doctor saying, "You are in time, just, she wants you to witness a death-bed codicil to her will and Catharine you had better stay here too, you will also be a witness."

They came to her bedside and Michael presented the document to her for her to sign. He had wrapped it around her Bible to give her something solid on which to write. Lying on her back she found it somewhat difficult. After her, the others signed, with the document still wrapped about the Bible, thus making it as legal as they thought was possible with the signature of three witnesses.

Anne Marie Majoribanks Anne Marie Majoribanks.

Signed in the presence of Father Michael Kennedy and in the presence of us who have herewith subscribed our names.

Joseph Meek .... Doctor

Cathleen Hannaway .... Ladies maid.

Michael Kennedy .... Priest

But, Michael had not written, "public exhibition in St Anne's Cathedral," he had written, "public exhibition at Holy Rosary Church," and that transgression had been his secret, haunting him for the twenty years. With the will wrapped around the Bible as they each signed, and the urgency of the moment, only Michael knew what the codicil said, and Her Ladyship had unquestioning trust in Michael.

Now, in October 1986, he was preparing to conduct a memorial service for Lady Marchbanks. He was wistfully looking at the Madonna, feeling and thinking how humbled he was in its presence. The mental and emotional responsiveness that he felt towards it brought him near to tears, all the time fingering his rosary, which was a present from Lady Marchbanks. She had had it blessed for him, by none other than the Pope himself.

His greatest fear, above that of God's wrath, was that, in conversation, he may let something slip and give his secret away to the Bishop.

In all those years he had not been able to truly confess his sins, always leaving out the big one. He knew that if he did not repent all of his sins he should not take communion. In consequence he should not have taken communion, but how could he avoid it? The Bishop would surely notice. Thus he was piling sin upon sin. Worse still, how could he absolve others' sins? Did those who confessed their sins to him actually receive the absolution that they desired? And what about the hundreds of masses that he had conducted, offering up the host so many times, how far into Hell was he to descend? Had he been struck off, "The register", and had he sent hundreds of souls to the other side, burdened with sin? Even Lady Marchbanks, she would have been the first. He often pondered why God had not visited him with some awful affliction? But then he also postulated that as God had not brought some terrible catastrophe upon him, there must be a divine reason. On the contrary, even though the Bishop had been petulant at the disclosure of the will. The Bishop had been of the understanding that the entire estate would fall the Cathedral. Nevertheless Holy Rosary and its Madonna had attracted so many devotees and revenue for the diocese that Father Kennedy was promoted to Monsignor. His God did not seem to be displeased with him.

Michael knew that right back in the Bible there were recordings of sins, which he considered far worse that his, but then, who was he to judge the ranking of sins? There was Lot who slept with both of his daughters; and Abraham used his wife for personal gain. Then there was David who had Uriah deliberately killed so that he could have his wife Bath Sheba; the progeny of which was Solomon. Mary did not get stoned to death as the law said she should. The supreme sinner was Judas, yet his part in the eternal scheme was probably more important than was Peter's. Someone had to do it. It might be that in the execution of the vast eternal plan the letters of the law could be overruled or bent.

He argued with himself: as Lady M. had not made any provision for the maintenance of Holy Rosary in her will, it would surely now be in ruins. The estate's workmen had long ceased their care of Holy Rosary. But as it happened, Michael's duplicity had kept the pews full of people from far and wide who benefited as a "Quid pro quo," by giving them a chance to see the Madonna. He was sure that Lady M. would approve of his correcting her omission and thereby ensuring the present, healthy financial and physical state of Holy Rosary.

He constantly hoped against hope that perhaps, God was not so disapproving of his actions. It is said, "God moves mysteriously his wonders to perform." So, while Lady Marchbanks had her free will to do whatever she chose with her finances. Michael might be just an instrument in God's mysterious way of correcting Lady Marchbanks' omission.

* * *

CHRISTMAS SHOPPING

A thing I find exhausts and shocking,
Is an expedition of Christmas Shopping.
You walk and walk until you drop,
But you must visit every shop.
It doesn't matter if cash is tight,
Plastic makes it all seem right.
Jimmy wants a Nintendo game,
Mary's wants are just the same.
Auntie Jean wants lots of smellies,
Uncle George will get some wellies.
We've lots of food, but get some more,
My feet are aching and getting sore.
I think I'll get a cup of tea,
But that has made me want to pee.
There are no toilets hereabout,
I don't think I can last it out.
We've one more present yet to buy,
If I don't pee, I think I'll die.

* * *

AND YET ANOTHER HIAKU

Nights are drawing in,
Autumn leaves are falling fast,
Summer did not last.

MODEL PICTURES

Gary was a man who was well set in his ways and habits, having had thirty-three years to consolidate his pompous attitude. He was a real, 'Johnny Know All', and he really did know it all, in respect of photography. Not many people, especially those of the opposite sex were willing to cling to him in any positive way. There was nothing physically abhorrent about him, but he was a social bore. He was very good at his chosen profession of Commercial Photography. He talked incessantly about it. In his photographs he could make a tinned rice pudding look fit to eat or make 'Utterly Butterly' look like butter.

He was not very proud of his abode which, though well appointed, was a two roomed flat with a not too picturesque aspect of a railway yard. It did sometimes afford a sighting of a classic engine such as the Coronation Scot, but the background scenery in his pictures would never come near the famous, 'It's the goods' picture in the old Guinness advert.

Once, and it might have been 'bad luck', he won a photographic competition. Since then he had been hooked. He lived on the small bit of fame that he gleaned from that success. He constantly dreamed and fantasised at being the top photographer among the beauties that tread the cat walk. He disliked anyone taking his photograph, thinking he was not photogenic, and he, above all, should know.

One particular day, to his annoyance, he had been cornered into having his photo taken by a woman. Her camera was minuscule, probably digital he surmised, with only one digit. This stupid woman with her diddy camera had not paid any attention to the background with its hanging towel and tea cloth, an ill-arranged dying plant and a fridge. Then in the foreground was a table full of empty glasses. To crown it all she wanted him to, 'smile!' He thought, "Idiot, get on with it."

He had a photographic eye; he should have been born with one camera lens eye in the middle of his forehead, just like the Cyclops.

While he waited for the flash which never came, he became aware that she was a classy dresser, and, when she moved the camera which, with her hands, had obscured her face, he thought, "not a bad—looker either."

Inviting herself, she sat the table and said, "This photograph will be worth a fortune one day. Can I buy you a drink?"

"You mean that 'Snap' will never be worth the taking, but as a fee for being a model I am worth a drink."

After ordering the drinks she repeated her claim as to the worth of the 'Snap' and said, "Stubbornly opinionated though you are, I have sought you out to make you a proposition."

Somewhat interested he asked, "What kind of proposition?"

"Hopefully financial," she said, as she carefully placed the camera into a leather pouch and into her handbag.

Noticing this, he thought it an expensive pouch for a trifling camera and became interested enough to ask about it.

"Oh that is part of my accoutrement; you are going to show me how to get the best from it."

"For a fee?" he questioned.

She pointed at him and said firmly, "You will get a great fee,"

"You are beginning to sound better than you look," he said, as his body language changed from an excessively relaxed posture in his chair to sitting up with elbows on the table, "Tell me more."

She told him that she was going to be the best *haute couturier* in the business.

"Wow," he said, "Who's opinionated? Yves St Laurent, rend your rags."

She ignored his jibe, passed him the tiny camera, and continued by telling him that with the camera she took clandestine pictures from the great fashion houses but had found that she needed tuition and practice so that she could take photographs and not, as he called them, snaps. It was useless to steal any of their ideas outright unless you are wholesale dressmaking, but some bits of their ingenious or imaginative secrets, if obtained before they hit the cat walk, could be usurped to advantage. Then she changed her body language to leaning on the table and, with great enthusiasm, explained the deal. She had been more than two years producing more than two dozen creations and had convinced a backer to sponsor a show, but unfortunately not in a recognised fashion establishment. She could not afford a photographer and even though this was not his usual line of work, she was sure that he would do her designs justice and she had no doubts that the whole thing would be a momentous success.

She then assured him, "The 'Snaps' you take will be in Vogue and all the society magazines. Are you in any way interested?"

Passing the camera back to her he said, "That, Miss what's your name? Sounds like I scratch your back and you scratch mine. It's an offer I can't refuse. When do we start?"

"Cathleen with a C. she said, "The show is on September 10th. My creations don't leave my premises until the day of the show. I have room for a photographic studio at the back of my workshop and we can start fitting it out now."

On the evening of October 1st, three weeks after the show, they were celebrating at El Dearoes restaurant. While Cathleen was adding and subtracting from a list that she had made on the cover of Vogue, Gary produced and was studying the original photograph of himself that Cathleen had taken,

Gary chided her for writing across one of his photographs. "I'm glad you are writing on the cover picture and not the one on page fourteen. I'm sorry that my best shot was not of your best creation, but the best picture is the one on page fourteen."

She looked up and involuntarily pointed the pen at him, "That's just why I came to you, you are so pernickety about your 'Snaps.' and I am so fastidious about my creations."

"Oh!" he chided her again, "Mine are snaps, and your rags are designer creations."

She knew he didn't mean it and confided, "This is all a haze. I have formal agreements for the franchise of twenty-one designs. If we don't get someone interested in the others soon, now that your photographs are in the public domain, they will be manna for the pirates. Someone in Morocco or India or even a back street in Bradford will copy them. Anyway when I bought this copy I saw you buy three copies of this rag; one Cheshire Life and two of Tattler."

Fingering the photo he said. "When you took this photograph five months ago, you were so sure that it would all turn out like this, and it has."

She said, "I'll tell you little story." and began telling him of a school teacher who had filled her mind with these positive ideas. Cathleen had mentioned to the teacher that she had little use for maths or other lessons, as she was going to be a dressmaker like her aunt. The teacher had said, derisively, "Only a dressmaker, why not a dress designer?" This sounded, to Cathleen like a good idea so she had agreed, "Ok, I'll be a dress, designer." Then the teacher pushed harder and suggested that a dress designer of any worth would need to go to Paris, Italy, New York or other foreign places to show her designs and sell them. This teacher then added that anyone in that circle who could not speak French or perhaps Italian would not make it in *couturier* business. Cathleen admitted she had never heard that word and it was the first French word she ever learnt. The teacher explained that handling money was another must to be learned, she suggested that Cathleen would not be making and selling mere 'frocks' she would be creating dresses that may cost hundreds of pounds, and what would the materials costs?. Since that goading she had become a model pupil in Art & Design, modern languages and business studies.

She chewed the thought in her mind saying, "That teacher filled me with high-octane fuel;—and, getting back to the back scratching, yes, the back scratching has benefited us both. Do you have any regrets?"

"No," he said, raising his glass, "I'm delighted, but do you think there's any chance of my ever being promoted to back—stroking?"

She gave a slight nod as if thinking and, raising her glass she replied, "Possibly! I'll make you a promise. I'll start tomorrow to design a backless, strapless *Chefs-d'oeuvre* for the occasion."
Masterpiece

BIRKENHEAD PARK

Birkenhead Park is the place to bring,
Your children, to get a taste of spring.
There'll be some snowdrops here and there,
And daffodils most everywhere.

See all the trees with their new clothes,
And frog-spawn in the lake's shallows.
Moles may have been busy making hills,
Blackbirds will show their nesting skills.

After winter all is fresh and new,
The swans and ducks will welcome you.
See a Heron catch a fish,
If you do then make a wish.

Each bird is busy to find a mate,
The thought of spring, I can hardly wait.

*   *   *

THE NORTH WIND

The North wind may blow,
And we may have snow.
But what will the aged do then?
Poor things.

While feeling quite chill,
They'll look at the bill,
And know they have knout in the bank,
Poor things.

They'll sit in their houses,
And cuddle their spouses,
And hope they won't freeze before spring,
Poor things.

"South of the border, Down Mexico way."

The rain was beating down in stair rods while three ten-year old boys, Harold, William and Michael, with broken voices were caterwauling, ".That's where I fell in love."

They were sheltering from the rain, sitting head to tails, feet or back to the front door, in the hallway of a three-up-and-cellar in Toxteth, Liverpool.

A flash of lightning that seemed so near streaked above the roofs; the singing stopped as they waited for the thunder, Bang, bang, bang, bang, bang.

"Why," asked Michael, "did the thunder come after the lightning?"

"Because," said Harold, "it takes longer for sound to travel than it takes for the light to travel."

William added his bit of knowledge, "You can tell how far away they are by checking the time between the flash and the bang."

"Well, how far away was that," asked Michael.

"I don't know but you can measure it," said William defiantly.

Harold offered, "I will tell you exactly." He got to his feet to fetch a brown school exercise book from the house. On the back of his book was all manner of mathematical information: weights and measures; metric and imperial; lengths and areas, in fact everything. He opened the parlour door to allow some light into the hall, and read, "Velocity of light 186,325 miles per second, Velocity of sound in air at 60°Fahrenheit, 1 mile in five seconds approximately."

William intervened, "So if there were five seconds between the flash and the bang it would be one mile away."

Harold corrected him, "Well not exactly, but near"

"There's another," said Harold, "one, one, one, two, two, two, three, three, three, three, four, four, four, five, five, five, six, six, six, seven, seven, seven."

Bang, bang, bang, went the thunder. "Seven seconds, that makes it nearly one and a half miles away," said Harold.

"There's another," William counted, "Eleven seconds."

"Yes about that," said Harold, "that means two and bit miles away, it's going farther away."

All fell silent and waited for the next flash, but it was a long time coming.

Michael's concentration waned, and he said, "It is duck-apple night soon."

"Yes, Saturday is Halloween," William answered, "the ghosts walk then."

"There are no ghosts! That's rubbish," Harold said scornfully.

"I bet you would not go past the Cathedral cemetery when it is dark on Saturday night," Michael wagered.

"What do you bet and I will," Harold said bravely, "make it worth my while."

"Will you go *into* the cemetery?" Michael raised the dare, "Go into the cemetery and I will bet you sixpence."

"OK, anyone else want to bet me sixpence?" Harold enthused with bravado.

"I'll bet sixpence that you won't go into the cemetery because you will have to climb the railings," William countered.

"I can go through the broken railings," Harold sneered.

Michael was disputatious, "If you go through the broken railings you will have to go down the tunnel to get to the cemetery! I'll bet a shilling that you won't do that!"

"For one and sixpence I will go down into the cemetery on Saturday night," avowed Harold.

Next day it was all over school. Tom Pollard a school bully said he would also bet a shilling and his toady Frank Jones offered three pence, but both queried whether Harold had money to cover the bets if he failed to go.

Harold replied to all, "I don't need the money because I *will* go; I am not frightened of ghosts."

Even Mr Bassett, the favourite teacher, heard about Harold and his bet. He urged Harold on saying, "There is nothing to be frightened of in a cemetery and you have a chance to make a few bob." He knew Harold to be a bright entrepreneur, always swapping and dealing until somewhere along the chain he swapped for money.

There were so many wagers that William and Michael were conscripted to help Harold with his book-keeping.

William made a suggestion to those gathered, "What I will do is write the names of those who are going to bet in my book, and you will all give me your money on Friday. Some of us will go with Harold on Saturday afternoon and put a copy of Saturday's Daily Post somewhere in the cemetery. Tom Pollard can write his name on it to be sure Harold brings back the same Daily Post. You *can* write your name, can't you Tom?"

Tom made a fist towards William and said, "I'll bet him five shillings but I want to come on Saturday afternoon."

"So do I," said Toady.

The agreement was reached and Mr. Bassett, who was on playground duty, watched from hearing distance.

Friday school finished and the tally was two pounds eighteen shillings and seven pence. Saturday afternoon came and William had the Daily Post ready for Tom to write on it. To remove any possible doubt William and Michael also wrote their names but they added, 'Good Luck Harold.'

They did not have to walk down the tunnel as the main gate at the near end was open, but, having walked the length of the graveyard, they looked up the eerie tunnel. The cemetery was in an old, sandstone quarry, the floor of which was some seventy feet below the adjacent, now famous, 'Hope Street'. There were iron railings high on the rock face of three sides of the cemetery. On top of the fourth side, high above the Cathedral was under construction. Its cruciform shape was clear with its side chapels complete and the scaffold-clad tower rising high above. Even in daylight the whole place was suggestive of the mysterious and supernatural.

There were two entrances which had enormous double gates. From one end there was a seven-foot-high and five-foot wide tunnel leading down from street level to the floor of the quarry. Along the walls of the tunnel there were grave stones, with names and dates, placed in the walls. It was supposed that there were coffins in the walls of this tunnel. At the bottom there were hundreds of graves, mostly of people who were buried in Victorian times.

The Hope Street side had sloping terraces. These were large terrace slopes from the days when the quarry was in operation. They would have been the zig-zag road over which the sandstone was extracted. There were burial chambers in the face of the rock on the terraces. Their arched and walled up entrances formed mausoleums of Victorian dignitaries. These mausoleums were spaced at ten foot intervals.

Famous people like Huskison and Abercrombie had more elaborate mausoleums down at the lower level which was accessed by a wide road to allow funeral coaches to pass in both directions, and gravel paths ran between groups of graves.

There were hundreds of graves, and even though they were mostly over one hundred years old, there were some with new flowers, but most had jars of dead flowers. The boys spent some time debating a suitable place for the newspaper. Eventually it was decided to jam it into an empty jar, on a grave that had a worn headstone inscribed, where it could be read, "In memory of Captain ??? Who fell near Kabul August 4th 1843 while serving under Lord Ellenborough." This grave was about twenty yards from the tunnel.

Harold agreed to the place for the paper and they all left the cemetery. As they passed the gate house an old, very old, lady came out to see what mischief the five boys were doing in the cemetery. She stood and watched them. As they passed, her eyes followed them. She was hunched and had silver-grey hair. She wore a black shawl and a long black dress. A cat stroked from side to side, polishing its jet black fur on her ankles. To the boys she was enough to frighten them even in daylight. Harold put on a show of defiance but he too sped up to get past the gate house.

They all returned to finish the arrangements outside Harold's house, some sitting on the steps and some leaning on the railings that were around an area which allowed light to the cellar window.

Harold holding court, leaned on the railing and said, "The newspaper says that the sun sets at five thirty-seven, so I will start from here at a quarter past seven, it should be dark by then. You can all be here to see me go, or you can come with me to the cemetery gates. From there I will go on my own."

Michael, who lived fifty yards along the street on the opposite side, turned to go home saying, "I will be here, I will go to the gates with you, but I'm not going down that tunnel with you."

The others dispersed leaving Harold and William alone. William stayed with Harold giving encouraging chatter until Harold's mother called him for his evening meal.

At a quarter past seven Harold was ready with a big torch. William and Michael were there, so were several punters, but Tom and Toady were not in attendance.

The three boys waited ten minutes and then left for the

cemetery. They arrived at the broken railings near one of the gates. Fortunately the gate was open. The Cathedral builders were using this entrance and area as a work-site. It must have been left open. It gave Harold an unrestricted path to the tunnel, albeit being some 50 yards from the gate and banked with trees. He picked his way along the path to the tunnel, trying not to use his torch in case anyone seeing it might think that grave robbers were about their business, stealing lead or artefacts from coffins. Michael and William had been most sympathetic; they had assured him that no matter what, they would be here at the gate when he returned. They knew he would not give up and would have cheered him on if all was not so dark and quiet.

Harold was now not so sure that there were no ghosts. After all, it was Halloween. He hesitated at the tunnel entrance, took a deep breath and said in a quiet voice, "Don't come near me you ghosts or you will be sorry." This gave him confidence and he started smartly down the tunnel with his light showing him the floor, but trying to avoid letting the light fall on the grave stones in the walls. The floor was paved with blue, brick-sized tiles. They were evenly laid but one must have been uneven. Harold's foot found it. He stumbled to the floor, the torch fell from his hand and the light went out. He lay on the floor for a second or two thinking, "I am not hurt." He tried not to think, "I am frightened," but he did think, "where is the torch?" In the blackness, he lifted himself to his knees and began to grope about. "I must do this systematically," he thought and began to sweep from side to side as he went down the tunnel. The night was cold but he was sweating marbles, his heart was racing and his hair was tingling. It occurred to him that it might be standing on end. Another though crossed his mind, "I hope this tunnel is not a route used by dog lovers." He felt a little relieved when his fingers touched the torch. He stood up and tried the switch. Up down, up down, went the switch, but no light appeared. He was now near to panicking. He unscrewed the bottom and screwed it back again. He banged the torch on his hand. Wow! It stopped being temperamental and gave forth what seemed a blinding light. His panic however, had not subsided. He reached the bottom of the tunnel taking great care not to stumble again.

When he emerged at the bottom his eyes had become accustomed to the darkness and high up in Hope Street, above the terraces, five street lamps shed their weak light right down to the floor of the cemetery. He soon found the jar in which the newspaper had been placed. Fear nearly over-took him again, but he grabbed the paper, screwing it up and pushing it up under his pullover. He also picked up the jam-jar, deciding that it would make a great weapon with which to fight the ghosts, if there were any.

He heard a noise of crunching on the path which petrified him. His whole body seemed to tremble but he instinctively turned his torch towards the sound. He was comforted when he saw that it was the seat of a rope tree swing that was moving in the breeze and banging against a headstone.

He reached the entrance to the tunnel and braced himself, took a deep breath and marched bravely up the tunnel brandishing his big torch and jam jar. He even cast the light on some of the gravestones along the walls.

On emerging from the tunnel he was confronted by a white thing about fifteen yards away, half on the path and under a tree. It was man-sized and made noises of, 'whoo-ooo'. His courage drained from him. He had thought that once out of the tunnel and away from graves and tomb stones, there would be little chance of a ghost, but now there was one and he had to get past it. He was sure that it was indeed a ghost. All the stories he had heard about there being no such things as ghosts were evidently lies.

More whoooooing emanated from the hovering white ghost and more frightening did it become. Harold had only about 100 yards to go to reach his two friends. He wondered how fast ghosts could run. Comforting himself he had another thought, perhaps they can't run at all. But then it didn't matter whether they could run or not, it was standing there in his path.

More whoooooing, convinced him, but it might have been pure panic, that he should make a run for it. After all he had brought the jam jar as a weapon and he had his big torch. So he ran.

The ghost had another session of whoooooing, but Harold could not stop now that he had started.

As he approached the ghost he threw the jam jar at it, He was sure that he had hit it. It gave a groan and stopped waving about. A little nearer but almost simultaneously, Harold threw his big torch. He was so near to the ghost that it might just as well be a truncheon stroke. At less than two yards it could not miss. It struck at what would be the head. The ghost went down in a heap as Harold raced passed. He forgot all about tripping, he covered the last 100 yards fast enough to break the four-minute mile record. The whoooooing had changed to a howl of someone in pain, but in the heat of those moments it never occurred to Harold that ghosts should not feel pain.

The two boys who had been dutifully waiting could hear the whoooooing and the howls, but they, being bathed in the glow of the argon street lamps, felt immune from ghostly attention. Nevertheless, the sounds of whoooooing and howling put a great stress on their allegiance to Harold and they were about to abandon their post when, out of the cemetery darkness, came Harold, running fast and as he passed, he gasped, "Come on quick, let's get away from here." The two boys did not ask questions but took up the pace of Harold. Neither of them slowed down until they had reached the bright lights around the Cathedral's main entrance. They puffed their way home while Harold babbled uncontrollably about the ghost and the loss of his torch, and how he had, bravely, thrown a jam jar at it. He still had the Daily Post tucked up under his jumper.

Back at Harold's house they sat on the front step while Harold recounted his Ghostly encounter, until each of them were called home. Another topic of conversation was the absence of Tom Pollard and Frank. If those two did not see that the newspaper had been retrieved that night, they might try to claim that Harold had obtained it at first light next morning. This possibility ruled out William's suggestion that they go to retrieve the torch next day.

The next morning Harold, sitting on William's front steps, was calmly and boastfully able to retell and retell the story of his brave adventure to his two friends and a slowly gathering audience. His valiant, "Daring-Do," jam-jar missile propulsion, grew more confrontational at each telling.

Harold relieved his two friends of their debt and suggested that William to hold on to the money.

The approach of Mrs Pollard and Frank broke up the gathering. The audience dispersed, leaving the three boys to face a torrent of abuse hurled at them by Mrs. Pollard.

"What have you done to our Tom?" She yelled.

"He is in the hospital with six stitches in his head and might have a broken leg because you threw a jam-jar and a torch at him."

All became clear to the three boys. Harold instinctively said,

"I didn't."

She, with her anger rising replied, "Don't say you didn't, because Frank here saw you."

Harold's mum, Mrs Evans, came out to see who was disturbing the peace of a Sunday morning and why.

"Did you do it Harold?" she asked.

"Yes," said Harold, who was now more frightened of his mother than he had been of the ghost in the cemetery, "but I thought it was a ghost. Granddad once told me that if I saw a ghost I should throw something at it and it would go away. So I did."

"What's all this about ghosts?" asked Mrs Evans.

Harold was stuttering. William took over, and told about the ghost and the Daily Post but not about money and the bets.

This put Mrs Evans on Harold's side, and, speaking from a position of advantage, she retaliated, saying, "It seems as though your Tom got what was coming to him. I hope he gets better but don't you come here blaming my Harold for your Tom's stupidity."

Mrs Pollard turned to confer with Frank but he had disappeared. She sheepishly agreed to go and ask Tom what really happened, but she did not return.

At school on Monday Tom was marked absent, him being in hospital, while Harold was a hero retelling his adventure to all who would listen, including Mr Basset.

William showed the newspaper to the punters and gave the money to Harold.

Harold took two pounds ten shillings and allowed his two friends to keep the rest.

Mr Bassett had Harold formally tell the class all about his adventure and then Mr Bassett asked them all to write their own story about Ghosts.

He confided with Harold, "I knew that you would do it because, as we know, there are no Ghosts in cemeteries and that was not a bad night's work, lad. Not a bad night's work at all."

* * *

"Where in hell is he?"

Mike was talking to himself whilst walking up and down the deserted pier in an effort to keep warm. His job on the pier, which was part of the harbour wall, was that of refurbishing a small shop, which was to open under new management at the start of the new season. He had arrived on time, having braved the 500 metres of wind-swept pier, but had to be 'inclined' to do so. His boss, Frank, who had the keys, was keeping him waiting on this cold and windy February morning. "If he doesn't come soon I'll be dead with hypothermia," he moaned.

He eyed the new door which they had fitted on the previous day and thought, "At least we will be out of the cold now that new door is in." The old door could be seen through the murky window with its melancholy sign "Back in five minutes." I hope that is not Frank's idea of five minutes.

His eyes searched the distant promenade in an effort to identify Frank's car.

Fastened to the pier with long, umbilical cords were all sorts of boats, bobbing and straining at their fetters. Other boats were crammed together, in relative safety, high on the slipway or sand at the back of the harbour. Waves crashed and stretched to reach them, making them pull on their lines when an odd wave tried to suck them back with it into deep water as it receded. Other waves crashed and beat at the promenade wall as they ran along its length, seeking a weakness. Cars on the prom were receiving an environmentally-friendly, salty wash.

At the end of the pier, the wind lashed at the canopy surrounding the theatre. It was now disused, but in the past, before the war, every year the 'Fol-de-rolls' concert party gave inferior performances to aged summer visitors. There was also a bar to which the wind showed no compassion. Unfortunately the bar was closed at this time in the morning and season. He thought of the many times, which seemed to be so long ago, that he had carried his pint out of the stifling, hot bar to lean on the rails of the pier and enjoy the summer breezes.

He cast his eye again over the shop. The weather beaten sign above the window read 'Cholmondeley's, Sweets Tobacco and

Fancy Goods' and he thought, "We have to erect a new sign, but I hope that Frank does not decide to do it in this weather.

Whilst musing thus, a van pulled up behind him and his boss jumped out, fumbling for the right key among some fifteen others. Safely inside the shop, his boss said, "I know, I know, I' should not bring the van up here but I'm not walking in this weather.

We should be able to finish stripping the place today but with the

door shut the dust will suffocate us."

"I would rather be suffocated than be frozen, but then, you didn't get frozen this morning did you?" Mike countered, and with that he levered away some of the tongue and grooved dado boards. As tea break approached he tackled the window seating, which was much cracked and worse for wear, having endured a century of summer suns blazing on it and the dampness of 100 winters. Below the boards there was a century of dust, deposited during those summers and winters. Then "What's this?"

Mike had found a faded, but originally blue, envelope. No! A letter. It was moulding, damp and disintegrating. He carefully extracted the pages from the envelope and read to Frank, who was now, with hammer in hand, looking over his shoulder.

"6 September 1939. My Dearest Georgina, Although the front sign read 'Back in five minutes', I waited and waited and waited all afternoon, but not a glimpse of you my darling. You are always in the shop on Wednesdays but alas not on this day, the worst day of my life. I must see you, to tell you how much more my love for you has grown. Now that I am going away I may not get a chance to see you or hold your hand for months. One kiss, just one before I go, would have put me in much higher spirits. Your father briefly attended to the shop but you know I could not ask him where I might find you. Why does he dislike me so much? I am writing this in old Harry's storeroom at the theatre. He has kindly supplied the writing material and you know he has always been our friend from the day of your father's tirade. Do you remember when Harry first turned a blind eye to us right here where I am now? I know that if you were here now, owing to the circumstances, he would have two blind eyes. Alas you are not. My heart aches to see you and I dread the future without contact with you. I have been instructed to report to an army medical centre in London. It is obvious that they will be requiring lots of doctors, and young ones at that, so it is my lot to be called. I must leave here on the 4:30 train. Harry has suggested that I can write to you via him at the theatre. This, my love, has cheered me a little. He has also offered to make this the first of his deliveries. I will write so many letters that the planks of the pier will be worn away between your shop and his storeroom. I must cease my writing lest I miss the train but, missing the train seems not so foreboding as missing you, dearest. I love you and will always love you, Ralph."

"Poor bugger" said Frank.

As they ate their lunch Frank did not pick his winners as he was accustomed to do, but they both considered who Ralph had been and if Georgina had any hereditary link to this shop. Where were they now? How might they start to find Ralph or Georgina?

"Start by looking for a local Cholmondeley," ventured Frank.

"We might start by finding who sold the lease to the new owner of this shop."

"Do it," Mike enthused. "Ring him tonight and find out."

"I will," Frank said, as he rose from his seat. "In the meantime start pulling more of these off, I am not paying you to take history lessons." Mike resumed the work but all afternoon they both conjectured on the life and times of Ralph and Georgina.

Next morning Frank was first on site, though the weather was no kinder. He could not wait to tell Mike his news. The new owner had confirmed that he bought the lease, this year, from a fourth generation of Cholmondeley who had operated here since the pier was built. "I've got Cholmondeley's address. It's about fifteen miles away in Haywards Heath. Get a move on and finish stripping this panelling. Get it on the van and this afternoon, after we have dumped it, we will make a fifteen mile detour to go and see him."

Mike taunted Frank as he set about completing the task, "Are you feeling sick? Did I hear that right? We are to go joy-riding on your time and using your petrol?"

Frank had no trouble finding the Cholmondeley house and eagerly rang the bell.

A man about 40 years old opened the door.

"This cannot be Ralph he's too young," Mike whispered.

Frank told the young Cholmondeley about the letter and they were both invited into the house.

"Mary," the man called, "come to hear this, or better, make some tea for our two guests; then come and hear this." The man was enthralled with the story and smiled or rather chuckled as he read the letter. "This would be Uncle Ralph and the letter is to Auntie Georgina. They are both in their eighties and live in Hastings, I never knew he was a softy like this."

Mary, his wife, heard the story and read the letter; "It has to be a letter to Georgina. I wonder how it got there."

Young Cholmondeley was as excited and interested as Mike and Frank, "We can't miss this, seeing their faces when they hear about finding it. Let's all make a date and I will arrange it so that we are there at their house, by chance of course, when you two arrive with the letter."

And thus it was set for Sunday afternoon.

Mike and Frank set out on the Sunday, eager to meet Ralph and Georgina. They arrived at a very large country house with sprawling gardens and long crunchy drive.

"Ralph must have a bob or two, this is some spread," Mike said as he came out of the car.

They could see young Cholmondeley's car on the crunchy drive, indicating that all was set for their introduction. No need to ring the bell, Mary came out to greet them and at the same time calling to Auntie Georgina. Mary's enthusiasm dispelled all pretence at it being a coincidental visit. Excitedly, Mary introduced Mike and Frank to a frail, white-haired, very spruce lady who came slowly into the hall from the side of an enormous central staircase.

She walked with the aid of a stick, and greeted them with a "How do you do?" Nevertheless, she was confused as to why Mary was eager to invite the strangers into her house.

Mike began with, "You must be the Georgina who sold tobacco and sweets on the pier before the war. We are both delighted to meet with you."

Still bewildered, she said, "Yes, but that was over fifty years ago."

"Ah!" interrupted Frank, "But fifty years ago, you had a secret tryst, and a secret hidey hole for your letters, you hid your letter in the bottom of the window?"

Her hand rose to cover her mouth as she said, "Oh! My goodness, yes."

There were smiles all round as Frank produced the letter, saying, "Would this, by any chance, be your letter? As he offered the mouldy envelope to her he said, "We were nosy and read it. We concluded that such a letter must have meant a lot to the owner?"

Mary surging with impatience said, "We invited these two gentlemen here to return the letter in person. We all want to see you receive it, and share with your most certain delight on its return to you, but of course we would very much like to hear it's story."

Georgina started by saying, "It was Ralph's letter really, he will want to know about it, but he has lately had a stroke and has difficulty forming his words." Nowadays, unless he is taken out in the car, he sits in the lounge admiring the garden."

Walking very slowly she ushered the four through a door that led from the magnificent hall, with its beautiful mahogany central staircase and a balcony, into the spacious lounge. Sitting by the fire was a white-haired gentleman; minus the jacket of what was obviously a bespoke suit, but wearing the waistcoat of it and his slippers. He too was initially bewildered at the entourage entering his lounge.

Georgina continued speaking as she walked to the window and pointed to the patio outside, "Or he sits out there in the sunshine, when we have any."

Frank opened with, "How do you do Mr Ralph?"

Ralph's lips moved but no sound came out but he nodded in acknowledgement.

Still clutching the letter, Georgina made her way to talk to Ralph. "Ralph dear, you remember that letter you left with old Harry on the pier in 1939?" She held the letter so that he could see it.

"Ralph managed "Yes—do." a stumble over some words that he wished to say and, "long time."

"Well dear, these two gentlemen have found it and brought it to us."

Ralph's hands made a slight movement as if to reach the letter and his eyes definitely lit up, but he stumbled over more words and all that came out were, "Me . . . . Read."

Georgina took out the pages and began to read to him, with her voice faltering and with both eyes tearful. At the end she said, "It was a lovely letter and I was heartbroken to have lost it. But I knew where it was." She placed the letter in Ralph's hand so that he could read it and leaned to kiss him on the forehead. She then turned to thank Frank and Mike saying, "How can I thank you for taking the trouble to find us. A simple thank you is inappropriate for the return of such a valued artefact, nevertheless I do thank you and am sure Ralph would be thanking you if he could. We must see that you receive some more tangible reward for your most valued and appreciated efforts."

Mary had made sure there would be tea and cakes and everyone settled as Georgina began her story.

"Ralph was a new young doctor at the local hospital. One night he and some friends were in the old theatre watching the show. The programme changed each week with visiting artists. Sometimes, if, after the first act, there was an empty seat. Harry would sneak me in to take the seat. One lucky night, that lucky night, the seat was next to Ralph. Seeing me without a programme he offered me his, and took every opportunity to make conversation about the performers. He left his friends to walk me home and subsequently made himself the errand-boy taking orders for sweets and tobacco for his patients, always buying from our shop.

We started keeping company. Dad who was a religious bigot eventually forbade me to see a protestant. Dad was steeped in Catholicism from, as he said, his ancestors from Normandy, and we stick to the old way. One day Dad found him in the shop and ordered him out, not to come back again. Of course we went on meeting because by then I loved him and he me. When it was cold Harry would let us in through the stage door to the theatre. We would sit back-stage or in his storeroom.

As if savouring the thought and repeating the experiences, she clasped Ralph's hand, which was still holding the envelope.

Now, on that day, three days into the war, most of the folk living or owning a business or property on the sea front were summoned without notice to go to the Town Hall. We did not know for how long, so we left the five-minute sign in the window. We were told that we had twenty four hours to remove anything that we valued. Dad and I then had only the next day to clear the shop as the pier was to be requisitioned by the army. They put a gun on the end of it. Nobody ever saw or heard it fired. All through the war we thought it was a dummy gun. I think the pier would have collapsed had it been real and actually fired! I did not return again that day as dad was arranging transport and the following day Dad was ferrying all the stock up to home.

Harry was now out of a job, but he hung around and chose his moment to deliver the letter to me that day, which was almost at the end of the twenty-four hours, and long after Ralph had left. I read it over and over and was not thinking when Dad returned. I was reading it by the window and fortunately saw Dad coming along the pier, so I tried to hide the letter in a crack of the window. Dad made only two more trips after that, and when Dad was not about, I tried but I could not get it out again. We left the shop, and my precious letter, but comforted by the belief in what everyone was saying, "It will be over by Christmas," We left the five-minute sign to patriotically state that we would be back."

"The day after that, the army commandeered the pier. Harry no longer had his address, he could not help us and not a letter reached me. The army requisitioned most of the houses in the town; they placed barbed wire and other defence ordinance on the prom which prohibited all civilians. Worse still, ours was one of the requisitioned houses and we were re-housed in the country near to where Mary and Edward live. Ralph had no chance of finding me." All the time her eyes were scanning the letter, but not reading it.

"Ralph went to France and at Dunkirk he chose to stay with the wounded that could not get away. As a prisoner of war he spent the rest of the war doctoring in a prison camp.

On his return he was well experienced in many fields of medicine, having, as a surgeon, pruned the limbs of many poor soldiers and nursed a lot of the lucky ones. When he was discharged he secured a post at St Bart's Hospital and spent his off duty days down here hanging around the pier, hoping to see me, but it was a long time before Dad could reclaim the shop.

His efforts were rewarded when Dad did get the shop back. Ralph followed Dad and found where we were living. I was overjoyed to see him again and our love was even stronger, such that I did not care what Dad thought and I did not go near the shop for a week. The only reason I did return was to try to get the letter but without destroying the new paint it was impossible. So there it lay for all those years. We never removed the five minute sign from the door; I hope it is still there.

Eventually Dad made his peace, having been given the choice of a total loss of his daughter or gaining such an accomplished son. Ralph and I were married. We came to live here where we brought up two good sons.

Edward's father, my brother died last year. Edward didn't wish to keep the shop, so he sold the lease."

Georgina put the letter in Ralph's hand. He gripped it and tried to open the pages, stumbling over the words, "Read myself."

Georgina opened the pages for him. He read it in silence nodding his head with an "Mm, mm," as he scanned the words. Oblivious to all who watched him in silence, near the end, he tried reading aloud and managed, "I love. you will. always. love."

Georgina's hand reached down to rest on Ralphs shoulder, as Ralph trying very hard concluded, "And. I do."

*   *   *

THE HUSTINGS

When it comes to time for voting,
And the candidates are touting,
For your vote and you haven't got a clue.
Don't fall prey to their emoting,
But unscramble their misquoting,
Their appetence is not for me nor you.

To get a raise in their annuity,
And knowing their veracity,
The PM allowed all noses in the trough.
They voted, all in unity,
To give themselves immunity,
From redress for the money they'd hived off.

They will promise earth and heaven,
But before the sun has risen,
They'll retranslate there every weasel word.
Every promise is forgotten,
To the core most of them are rotten,
We will never realise the hopes we shared.

You must do your civic duty,
But don't cross co's she's a cutie,
Or handsome chap who bucks your oestrogen.
Most are in it for the bootie,
So forget about their beauty,
You must try to find some really honest men.

Oops! Or women

Scene: in a public house. Two Ronnie's style.
Two drinkers: George and Walter,

George   Did you read about that feller who won 13 million quid on the lottery?

Walter   Yes. Silly bugger said it wouldn't change him.

George   Well of course it wouldn't change him, he'd be the same as he always was, just like me. Well perhaps I have changed a bit, once I was thin and handsome.

Walter   Yes George, and now you are fat and less handsome.

George   What would be the first thing you'd do if you won Walt?

Walter   I would count it.

George   You don't get money you can count.

Walter   You don't get money you can count?

George   No you get a cheque and take it to the bank.

Walter   Then I'll go to the bank and count it. I'd tell them to have it all stacked in £50 notes.

George   They wouldn't do that for you, anyway do you know how many £50 notes there would be?

Walter   I suppose there would be millions.

George   No, they won't have your money in the bank.

Walter   Well where would my money be?

George   They lend it to people who want to borrow it.

Walter   They're not lending my money to all sorts of scroungers! Those scroungers can go and get a job to earn some money and not come borrowing mine. I would go and ask to see my money every morning. Just to make sure they don't hand it out to any old Tom, Dick or Harry.

George   No, Walt, the bank won't keep your money for you to see at any time that takes your fancy.

Walter   Well, on the telly the banks are always boasting how they will look after your money.

George   They do look after your money, but they don't keep it ready for you to see in crisp £50 notes.

Walter   What you are saying is that I never get to see my money?

George   Well . . . . Yes.

Walter   What's the use of winning then, if, when you win, you don't

	get to have money in the bank.
George	You do have money in the bank.
Walter	But you've just said I haven't. They take your money off of you and use it to *substitise* the *Hopra* house or the *Ballee* so that those '*ard* up toffs only have to pay 25 quid instead of the 50 to put their arse on a seat. Then when you get the numbers right, they give the money to the bank who give it away to anyone who wants to borrow it. I can see why that feller says it won't change *him.'cos* he never **gets** any money.

*   *   *

THE SAFETY OFFICER

My words are, look for danger day by day.
To keep your fingers where they ought to be.
Because I'm Safety Officer, that's my way.

I do all things the health and safety way.
I always wear official dungaree.
My words are, look for danger day by day.

I always try to keep the tears away.
Ensure my workmates go home for their tea.
Because I'm Safety Officer, that's my way.

If I let up, there'll just be hell to pay.
Short-cut ideas I cannot let run free.
My words are, look for danger day by day.

Maintain this stance with measures not half-way.
There'll be no accidental absentee.
Because I'm Safety Officer, that's my way.

Surgeons won't prune some bits away,
Or need posthumous words of thee to say.
My words are, look for danger day by day,
Because I'm Safety Officer, that's my way.

THE MAGIC SUITS

Around the middle of the century, last century not this century, there were two inventors who created an all purpose fibre. This could be made to look like twisted-woollen yarn and could be woven into cloth of any quality and texture. For example it could be made into Scotish plaid which looked exactly like Scotish woollen tartans. Another finely-woven, woollen cloth called Worsted could likewise be produced. It was even possible to produce materials similar to cloth made from a goat's hair which we call Mohair. Linen or Silk were the special types that they could simulate. It also had the facility to be made exactly like hair, human or an animal. Thus imitation fur coats and wigs could be made.

Other inventors had produced thread such as Rayon, Lisle, Nylon and all sorts of others. This new thread was just another polymer. The inventors knew the story of 'The Man in the White Suit.' In that story a man has a suit that does not need cleaning and never wears out. Laundry workers and tailors lost their jobs. Nobody liked the man in the white suit. If our two inventors were to make their fortunes with this new fibre, then the new clothes must not be like that of the 'White suit' and cause all that trouble. At the end of that story the fibres melted after nine months in sunlight and then the man had no suit at all.

The two inventors searched for a special or unique selling value for this new material. They noticed that most trades had either uniforms, sometimes called 'livery' or at least some special style or pattern to their working clothes. Chefs wear tall, white hats and black-and-white chequered trousers; butchers wear white aprons with vertical blue stripes and boater hats; artists are always pictured in a smock. This being so, the inventors hit on the idea of pretending that their invention had a very special magic ability.

They also knew the story about the cheating men who sold the Emperor his new clothes and told the Emperor that only very wise men could see them. Everyone said that they could see his fine new clothes because they did not want others to think they were not wise. But everyone knew that they could not really see any clothes at all on the Emperor and that the Emperor was naked.

Our inventors had to have a story that would really fool everybody. They decided that they must convince people that their material really did have special magical qualities.

After much thought they hit on a grand idea. If a person, man or woman, had clothes made of their special material, in the uniform or style of any profession it would automatically give the wearer the mental qualities of the highest intelligence and the ability that is expected of a person wearing the particular style of dress. For instance a person wearing a Barrister's or Judge's wig and gown which was made of their magical material would immediately get the brain and knowledge of the best Judge or Barrister in the land. A Field Marshal's uniform would make the wearer a genius of military strategy, and a pilot's uniform would make the wearer a Flying Ace.

Of course the inventors could not advertise this material as actually being magic on the television or in the newspapers, because it was not magic. They sold it in secret, always telling the buyers not to tell anyone else. It was supposedly difficult to obtain, always supposedly rare and always at a very high price. This was making the inventors very rich, especially in the USA.

Many silly people bought clothes or uniforms made of the magic material and believed that the clothes had made them clever. A great number of these were politicians. You know how politicians always think they are the only ones who can solve the troubles of the country or even the world. Even when things go wrong they keep saying that they were right. They in turn choose the men or women from among themselves to hold the highest offices in the land.

Now if someone who was chosen happened to be wearing a magic suit, he would of course be sure to think that the suit had made him wise enough to be chosen. In fact it shows that the chosen and the choosers were not necessarily clever at all. When ordinary citizens, without the special clothes, hear that the 'wise men' have been chosen by other wise men, they cannot but believe that their country was, and is, being run by very clever men. This was because the ordinary citizen could in fact see clothes on the persons and could not see a person's brains. (This was unlike the Emperor, who could be seen to be not wearing any clothes at all.)

Ordinary citizens are a mixture of wise and not so wise persons. We are all are confused when it comes to voting time and the genuine wise man may not get many votes.

Of course all those who believed in the magic powers were in no way clever, or they would not have believed such rubbish. But not wanting to appear less clever than others, they secretly bought the clothes and all convinced themselves that the suits or uniforms made a difference. So in a way it was like the Emperor's clothes.

Lots of newspaper editors bought suits made of the magic material. You can tell this by looking at the things they write in their newspapers, very often not reporting the news but filling the papers with their supposedly 'wise' opinion of how things should be. There is often quite a lot written on supposedly important people, especially who wears what. Need I tell you more about newspaper editors?

There are some would be Generals. Generals need wars to be effective. Without a war they cannot get promotion or be made a Knight or a Lord. They convince the politicians (some of which as I have said, wear the special magic clothes) that there are enemies everywhere, and so foment wars.

Artists were some of the most dumb. Some of them bought their special shaped (like a tent) overalls. Oh! how they babble on about abstract expressionism; conceptual art; post modernism and the true meaning of their 'action paintings,' and the heaps of rubbish that they insist is art. The clever and wise 'You know who,' with the wisdom giving clothes, all agree.

Some business-men and women bought suits which they were sure would make them captains of industry. In turn they too, chose other men amongst themselves who they thought were clever. In turn the men they chose naturally thought themselves an intellectual cut above others. The chosen ones were promoted to be executives of great companies like the Telephone, Water, Electricity, Railway Companies; the hospitals and other such large corporations. But they are really sometimes lacking in know-how. They make such a mess; often thinking that they were making lots of profit when they were not. Banking men were particularly well disposed to owning the magic suits. They gave themselves high wages and large bonuses. Many companies were soon bankrupt or nearly so. Worse still, when the companies were ruined and near their end with not a lot of money left, some gave themselves even bigger wage packets stuffed with whatever was left of the remaining money This was of course because each one thought the other to be clever and copied their practices.

One of the most lucrative clothing items was, and is, football shirts. Hundreds and hundreds were sold and are being sold, for a rainbow of differing team colours. Who hasn't heard the self-opinionated spectators and armchair experts sounding off about the actions of real players? Some think that by wearing a magic shirt they, of course, know more about playing the game than Becks or Owen and Rooney. You have surely heard them. "Come on Becks, do this or do that," as though Becks, who does not need or have a magic shirt, does not know how to play football or what he is doing.

A group that should wear a clown's clothes because they are so funny are the DIY experts. Here I include the Interior Designers. See them on the TV. Suggesting colours for walls and curtains, for sure they can only be seen in 'hells rainbows'. They think that concrete can set almost before the programme has finished, whereas concrete really takes three or more days to set.

Now reading this you may, with a wry smile, think that there are some, at least one, would be, 'Short story teller,' who has had a special suit made for him. Perhaps you are right.

Much money is made from a group of men who buy red Father Christmas suits and white beards. When they put on the red suits and their beards they, believing the suits to be magic, think they are actually Father Christmas. These men, as I have explained, are really not Father Christmas but they are inclined to do nice things just like Father Christmas does. They do not do as much harm as those men who think they have magically become wise.

If you are in town visiting the shops when Christmas is near, you may think you have seen more than one Father Christmas. This may puzzle you. Don't be surprised. The reason is that when it gets near to Christmas all the men who think they are Father Christmas put on their suits and go to the shops to talk to mums and children. But you know and I know that there is only one Father Christmas.

When you see one of these other Father Christmases please do not tell them that they are not real, because they are not very clever and have paid a lot of money for their suits. It would be cruel to tell them, and if they are happy pretending and being kind, well, what does it matter, so long as we know the truth?

Agnes had been last in the queue when God was handing out good looks and body shapes. She could most adequately be described as a cross between Margaret Rutherford and Joyce Grenfell. She had worked for the County Council for 35 years before taking early retirement. Not quite, she contended, which was more to the truth, that she had been constructively dismissed. She had never been propositioned by any of the male sex and now lived alone with her cocker spaniel. She did have relatives but they had turned out to be rather undesirable types: a sister, who was constantly in debt, had a husband who was a good provider, but alcohol had overtaken her senses and after much bickering and much unpleasantness, her husband left her with two children; a niece, who had incessantly sponged and bled Agnes of any financial resources, and a worthless nephew, who more or less demanded from her any surplus.

This nephew was a vicious-minded drop out, a petty thief who was into stealing cars and anything else that would bring him some money. He was not averse to rolling a drunk or beating up a foreign tourist. He had enjoyed two periods of Her Majesty's hospitality.

Agnes had been good at her job but was held back by being a not too pretty woman in a man's world. On leaving her grammar school, she had joined the Council with a group of seven sixteen-year-old school leavers, one of which, Bill, eventually progressed to be her line manager. Bill, and other male employees had progressed rather speedily, some transferring to other council offices and most of the female entrants had found themselves husbands.

The males, to a man, or rather to a youth, had 'Sexually harassed' the girls in the office. There had been 5 males in an office of 32 females. The office staff had, at that time, recently been restructured and the new staff had been recruited. Agnes and Bill had been among the new entrants.

The young bucks had enjoyed their harem of young females. Bottom pinching and sexual talk had been rife during their callow years. It had persisted as the young girls had left to marry and new staff had been employed. As the bucks progressed higher up the promotion ladder they had each realised that they must be more circumspect. Fraternising moved out of the office, but still persisted. Some staff progress reports were adjusted. Cases of unpunctuality and extra days of absence were shown a measure of leniency to favourites. Even Bill, her line manager, could engineer an extra day off for himself or others, with a few judicial strokes of the biro. Architectural moonlighting in office time was rife but, owing to her lack of sexual appeal, Agnes was not party, nor invited to be party, to this malfeasance.

The passing of internal examinations presented little difficulty to Agnes. She could keep up with her male peers, but, being a woman, and not being physically attractive to her womanising line managers, promotion had passed her by with a vengeance.

As time went on, the Bucks sought and gained promotion in other councils or departments, whilst Bill rose to near being the top man in the Office, without needing to relocate.

Agnes had lived near to Bill for years and in earlier days, when out shopping, had been introduced to his wife. Agnes had often seen and engaged Bill's wife in pleasantries about babies and the like. Unfortunately, unlike the other Bucks, Bill had inherited this one member of staff who knew all his past indiscretions. Agnes was, in his opinion, his Achilles heel and, since gaining a prime position of department head, he had made her life hell.

On the morning of her mother's death she had omitted to phone in and explain her reason for absence. Bill had made it his business to make a disciplinary case that would stick.

On another occasion he had barred certain staff, including Agnes, from overtime but when a local MP came making a late walkabout tour of the office with his 'Vita-Lampada' veiled, 'Vote for me talk', she, not being entitled to overtime, did not wait for the pep talk. She packed up at the appropriate finishing time and left the office, much to Bill's disgust. Somehow this was another case for discipline. Seemingly she was expected to do overtime for no reward.

Agnes had born this torment stoically, nursing her grievance and had not complained to any of her peers. More and more pettifoggery, nit-picking discipline cases had forced her to look for a way out. A way out which would keep her pension rights secure. She was sure that Bill would be vicious enough to deprive her of her pension rights if he could.

Out of the blue the call came for any who would like to take early retirement with enhanced pension rights; this was an offer not to be refused. She took the pension and placed the £24,500 lump sum in a bank account with the several grand she had managed to secret away from her avaricious relatives.

Her association with her nephew, Darren, was no happier. He would threaten her dog if she did not accede to his wishes and she would capitulate. He was forever breaking the law and would sometimes bring his stolen goods to be secreted in her house, which she had inherited from her mother. He had also demanded a duplicate key to the house. His two accomplices treated her with contempt and were unruly when Darren had invited them into her house although she had vehemently objected to having them near. He and his two companions stole cars to order. They sometimes drove as couriers or 'Bag Men,' on errands for a local drugs dealer. In order to frighten her they boasted to her about their escapades. Darren related how he or they had beaten up and robbed a Chinese man. They had also secreted a handgun in her loft. Once when she was trying to resist Darren's demands for money he fiddled with some bullets and placed the gun against her dog's head and threatened to kill it. She was in constant fear of him and of being implicated as an accessory in his nefarious enterprises.

As time went on, she nursed her fears of Darren and dreamt of ridding herself of his influence. Then one day Darren and his two criminal friends had called and taken the gun away. To her chagrin they had returned late that night with a holdall and boasting that they had ripped off one of Big Ben's couriers. They knew that Big Ben made deliveries and a collection Thursday nights. In fact the three of them had spent many Thursday evenings waiting to see if Big Ben would employ them to chauffer his 'Bag man'. Big Ben was a six-foot-tall, black man who dealt in drugs, prostitution and protection. He was emulating a Godfather.

Darren et-al counted out over thirty thousand pounds, and although boasting about their prowess, they were clearly afraid of Big Ben's retribution. If Ben ever discovered that it was them; he would surely kill them. They were sure that they had covered their backs with a master plan, boasting to Agnes that they had first stolen a car, a match to the one in which Darren usually drove. They had driven this stolen car to the heist, while Darren's car had been parked outside Agnes' house all night. This they claimed was the masterstroke. They put all the money and the gun in Agnes' loft, 'to cool,' and threatened to 'cut' Agnes, and her dog, if she touched it or told anyone about it. The three then settled down to drink from a twelve pack that they had brought.

At about 12.30 there was a loud excited banging on Agnes' front door. When Agnes opened the door, Big Ben and three heavies pushed past her and menacingly confronted the three 'Innocent' drinkers. Of course they protested their innocence, claiming and imploring Agnes to substantiate their claim that they had been there, drinking all night.

One of the heavies went out and returned saying that Darren's car was cold and had probably been there all night. This prompted Ben to say that the car that the hijackers had used was the same as Darren's and made a deduction that the three may have been innocent and someone else was trying to put the blame on them. Ben and his entourage left without spilling any blood, but they were in a blistering rage, they were mouthing many expletives in their description of what would happen to those who had stolen Ben's money.

The self-satisfaction and drinking of Darren and his friends continued until near three o-clock in the morning. They departed, leaving the empty cans strewn over Agnes's lounge.

While she was cleaning up after them, she thought, why am I plagued with them and suffering this life I have to live? She went to bed that night with the outline of an equally inspirational master plan, which the empty cans had given her. She seriously considered how she could rid herself of the thieves.

She brooded on this plan for weeks and every time she noticed the loft door she was stricken with fear but rehearsed the plan in her mind. As the plan matured it began to have ways which would include giving Bill his comeuppance.

The more she thought of the plan, the more ideas of how to carry it out came to her. She would start collecting information that she needed and if, in the end, she was too frightened to carry it out, there would be nothing wasted.

First she would examine the serial numbers on the bottom of beer cans to see if there was any sequence. There seemed to be a batch number and a sequence number that differed by one to its adjacent can in any four or six pack An adjacent or near pack would have the next four or six numbers, unless some shop assistant had been rearranging the stock.

Then she stalked Bill's wife to find her shopping habits. By periodically waiting in the café of the local supermarket store she was able to discover and hone this information of when Bill's wife would most likely be out shopping. Agnes watched what she bought, and on some occasions made it her business to make some conversation. She particularly wanted to see what, if any, cans of beer or Lager Bill's wife bought.

One day, nearing Christmas, after spending hours in the café, she was rewarded with the information she needed. Bill's wife was inspecting the beers and lager. Agnes moved to engage her in conversation. Agnes watched her carefully as she inspected the labels on various products probably to ascertain their alcohol content. She took two four-packs of Boddingtons saying, "Bill likes Boddingtons and Christmas is coming." After some thought, she took another two packs from the shelf. Then changed her mind again, and put one pack back on the shelf.

Agnes noted this and later when Bill's wife had moved away took care to select the same four-pack of Boddingtons that Bill's wife had first inspected. She had to be most careful not to touch any part of the cans even with her gloved hand. By lifting the pack beneath the desired pack, she eased the selected pack off the shelf and into her basket, without touching it. This was better than Agnes had planned, as she had only hoped to get Bill's wife's fingerprints on any brand can, but on cans with near numbers to, and of the brand that Bill preferred, was a bonus. At the till she feigned the need for help with loading the conveyor and with the packing. She noticed that the checkout girl hardly touched the actual cans as they were held it the plastic wrapper.

Agnes then returned to the café and 'coincidently' came out of the café just as Bill's wife was passing. Agnes directed the ensuing conversation to plans for Christmas and family matters.

Bill's wife said, "We are all going to spend Christmas and New Year with my parents in Shropshire, then Bill is coming home while the boys and I stay on till the weekend, Bill will have to cook for himself for a few days."

Agnes knew that both boys must be in their twenties and had left the home. One had been to a university.

Agnes nearly jumped for joy. This bit of information fitted one hole in her plan. As fortune had given her the valuable information about Bill's movements and being alone in his house, Agnes now knew the likely evenings when this would occur. She resolved there and then she would go ahead with her perfect crime.

At home she put the bags in a bin bag and put it in the shed as if it were rubbish. If Darren had found it, it would have been drunk.

The next major part of the plan was to go to the bank and draw ten thousand pounds in cash from her now thirty five thousand plus pounds of retirement money. She had never mentioned to any of her family that she had such a sum and never received bank statements, they would have inveigled it out of her. Before she entered the bank she rubbed her eyes until they were red and appearing to be sore. She forced herself to cry. This was difficult, but actors can do it, and if she was to be successful with her plan she had to cry.

There was a small queue in the bank. Having an audience was like having a cherry on top of her plan.

Noting her reddened eyes a woman asked, "Is there anything wrong my dear?"

"No," said Agnes and managed a few more tears,

At the counter Agnes handed in the cheque as she sobbingly said, "I want to withdraw ten thousand pounds in cash please."

The teller, surprised at the large sum confirmed, "Ten Thousand Pounds?"

"Yes" said Agnes "ten thousand" in a voice that could be heard by the next few customers.

The teller counted the bundles of one thousand pounds as he enquired, "You seem to be distressed, is there anything wrong. You look as if you have been crying?"

Again Agnes assured him and those about that there was nothing amiss and awkwardly stuffed the bundles in her handbag each bundle was wrapped with a paper strap just like those which Darren had stolen. Each strap was stamped and with what looked like a signature. All this time the rest of the queue were looking on.

At home she made sure that it was placed were Darren would not happen upon such a large sum of money.

Three days later she repeated the procedure. There were some little differences in the act but she managed to get the same teller. The teller remembered Agnes, he commented about the crying and the bloodshot eyes she had this time. That he should remember her was part of the plan and it was working. Three days before Christmas she took out another ten K.

Bill's detached house backed onto a railway, the small embankment and verge of which was overgrown with mature trees and some bushes. It was part of the plan to make sure that there was access from the railway so that she could approach the rear of Bill's house in the dark. To do this she took to walking her dog near the railway. With the dog she could stop and inspect without attracting too much attention. Here a part of her plan seemed impossible. She did not want to cross the electric lines in the dark but there was access to Bill's house from the opposite side of the track. The only other access to the track on Bill's side was 500 yards away at the station. She judged this distance by counting the houses from the station to Bill's house and multiplying it by a paced measurement of a house frontage. That was too long a walk to accomplish in the time she had imagined, she would have to adjust her timing. She did note the curtain arrangement of houses so that in the dark she would know when she was at Bill's house.

Agnes slept on the matter and ruminated for days. She realised that she could easily change her plan but if she was going to walk at the side of the track she must check the train times for the night of January the first. This she did and judged that she could, hopefully, walk the distance there and back, hiding in the trees, as trains passed. It must be without a light. Agnes spent a few daylight hours ostensibly waiting for a train at the station and took several rides on the train. She was all of the time getting the picture of the railway track-side in her mind.

All was set; it was Wednesday, Christmas Eve. Agnes went to her sister's house where she knew there would be a party. She took with her the two four packs of 'Boddingtons.' As she had hoped, Darren was present and so were his two accomplices. His mother and his sister, together with boyfriends and girlfriends made enough present to render Agnes unnoticeable as she now and then busied herself distributing, collecting and clearing cans very selectively. Nobody noticed, and she was sure that on the special rounds of issuing and clearing up she wore Marigolds, issuing and picking up very selectively.

The next night, when, as she had been told, Bill and his family would not be home, she made her trial walk up the railway from the station to the rear of Bill's home. She took with her a burglar bar that had been discarded by Darren. She was also wearing an old pair of Darren's boots. The intention was to make a hole in the fence big enough for her to get through, without snagging any of her clothes. All this was to be done without any light but her eyes became sufficiently accustomed to the darkness for her to accomplish the task. Bill had made it easier by making a gate in his back fence, such that Agnes had only to remove one slat from the fence, put her gloved hand through and slide the bolt. She stood in the shadows for some fifteen minutes surveying the garden in the light thrown from the neighbour's windows. She had to be sure that she did not fall in a fish pond or stumble over some other obstacle.

Twice since Big Ben had lost his money he had employed Darren's little gang. Agnes usually dreaded Thursday nights when they were in her house awaiting possible orders. Ben was lately doubling up on his protection and they were now in regular employ. At least that is what Agnes had gleaned from their idle talk. Christmas Day was a Thursday and it was business as usual. Agnes held great hopes that New Years Day being a Thursday it would be the same. They did not take the gun with them. In more idle talk they reasoned that they knew that nobody was going to rob them, also they dare not let Ben know that they had such a weapon.

New Years Eve came and went, with Agnes convincing herself that this was the last year of her suffering.

New Years Day she was on tenterhooks all day and evening. If the boys went on their errand she must be full of courage and do the deed.

All Friday night and the weekend she was unable to sleep. She scanned the newspapers and at midday on Sunday she heard, on the radio, "The police are investigating the death of a man who has been shot at point blank range. Mr William Sinclair was found this morning by his wife, who had returned from a stay with her parents."

Agnes was shivering with fright but she told herself that she must keep her composure. From now on she must act better than Julie

Walters. She had climbed into the loft and substituted her money for that which had been stolen from Big Ben. She then placed Ben's money in a waterproof bag which she had prepared and placed it in a hole next to the dogs bowl in the garden and prepared a large bone to be given to the dog when and if any police came calling. That would keep nosey parkers away from the dog's territory. She had carefully selected this resting place for the money. It had not to show any sign of recent disturbance. She hoped that the dog's clumsiness with the bowl and water followed by muddy paws would soon camouflage the area.

She waited impatiently for the next news bulletin, and was beside herself with torment when there was no further comment. If Darren came for his money now it might be catastrophic, though she doubted that he or they would notice any difference in the binding of the bundles. Rumours abounded that the police were everywhere, questioning everyone, appealing for information and most interesting, they had been seen searching the railway at the back of Bill's house. On the Monday her sister called in great distress to tell Agnes that the police had arrested Darren and his two mates. Agnes went to her sister's house to commiserate with her but inwardly she was thinking, "All is going to plan." She insisted on making tea for her sister while all the time she was full of fear that she would be found out.

Choosing her time and practicing her part she approached the most daring move of her game plan. She was about to put her head into the lions mouth but did not know if it would bite, however there was no turning back now.

She went out at night, trying not be seen. Nervously she rang 999 from a call box to ask for the person in charge of the Sinclair case.

She heard an officious voice say, "Detective Inspector Wallace speaking, how can I help you?"

She explained that she was Darren's aunt and went on to say, "I have information which might be of interest to you, but I do not want what I tell you and my name broadcast to all the police and newspapers. If you would quietly come to my house as though uninvited, I will co-operate."

Inspector Wallace and another officer were not long in coming. Agnes had now to be an 'Oscar winner' with her acting. She began in a faltering voice, which was interspersed with tears, "Darren, my nephew, has been tormenting me and extorting money from me for years."

The Inspector was very attentive and took copious notes as she related some of the instances of Darren's evil mentality. He asked whether Darren or his friends had been there on the New Years Day or since?

She told him they had been in her house and that Darren had done something in the loft and that the three of them had left at about seven o'-clock, but came back some time after midnight and seemed to be subdued. Darren had made another visit to the loft. They then left at about two or three o'-clock in the morning. She had not seen them since then.

She was asked if she had any knowledge about what Darren did in the loft.

"Not really," she replied "he has been using my loft as an Aladdin's cave, they have put all sorts up there and threatened me with my life if I go nosing. I know that he had a gun up there and there should be £30.000 in a red bag."

The Inspector, true to his word arranged an unobtrusive search of her loft where they found the things that Agnes had described. They also searched the rest of the house including the garden, where the dog showed its displeasure that someone might take his bone.

To her surprise and fright, the Inspector became officious and cautioned her saying, "What we have found might make you an accessory. Are you sure that you want to go on giving us this information, it might be used in evidence against you."

"I hope it won't be, but I do want to help you," she said.

The Inspector's assistant was trying to keep up, writing down everything that was said, although they had not said the usual 'Everything you say may be taken down,' etc.

The Inspector showed her the gun, saying, "You knew that this was up there?"

"Yes, he once held it to my dog's head and threatened to kill it if I did not give him some money."

"We have also found the sports bag, the bag you mentioned; it contains a substantial amount of money. You knew about that also?"

"It should be thirty thousand pounds, it is all mine." She said.

The Inspector, who, seemingly, had not registered the amount in his mind when she had previously mentioned the thirty thousand pounds, was taken aback by this the statement. "How come?" he asked?

She told him that Darren had found out about the money in her account when he found and opened a letter from the bank. It was an annual statement. He said he would kill the dog and cut me if I did not draw it out for him. He stood outside the bank while I went in to get it. He put it in the loft and demanded that I give him a key to my house so that he could come and go to his hoard."

Inspector Wallace took Agnes into his confidence saying, "We know this Darren, we put him away when he was sixteen for stealing with menaces from an old woman, and again when he was twenty three for GBH. If this gun turns out to be the one that killed Mr Sinclair, together with your evidence, he will be away for thirty years." The Inspector continued, "We were initially looking for Mr Sinclair's wrist watch and we suppose he had some money on his person when he was killed. But this lot is quite different."

After what seemed an eternity of other questions the Inspector and his Detective left, telling her he would be back and not to discuss their conversation with anybody especially not a newspaper. This suited Agnes just fine.

Four days later the Inspector did return and told tell her that Darren and his associates had been remanded in custody, and bail had not been allowed. They had checked her story about the money. The evidence of the wrappings and the teller showed that it had been drawn from her account. The teller also volunteered the information that he remembered that Agnes had been somewhat distressed when she made the withdrawal of these large amounts. Inspector Wallace assured her that it would be returned to her in due course. He also said that it had no bearing on the murder and would not be mentioned at the trial. He commented that, as it was discovered in her loft, it would be difficult to prove that Darren had extorted it from her as it was technically still in her possession.

Months later Agnes was to be called as witness against Darren. Her sister and her niece had not spoken to her for a month. She had to tell about the gun being placed against her dog's head and she made a great play about them taking the gun with them on several occasions, but she was not aware of when they last took it with them, except to say that she knew Darren had returned with something in the early hours of the second of January.

The Crown produced three lager cans which they had found in the bushes fringing the railway track. The police had found several sets of fingerprints on the cans and two person's fingerprints were particularly interesting. Each can had clear evidence that Mrs Sinclair had handled them. One can bore a clear overlapping set of Darren's fingerprints. Similarly another can bore two sets of prints, those of one of Darren's accomplices and Mrs Sinclair's. The third can bore only the fingerprint of the third accused and possibly the till lady's prints. Other cans of similar origin and batch number were found in Mr Sinclair's fridge. The prosecution claimed that these clearly showed that the cans had been taken from Mr Sinclair's fridge and the fingerprints proved beyond all reasonable doubt that at least two of the accused had been in Mr Sinclair's house to obtain them.

The gun was produced, and it had been established by the ballistics department that it had, indeed, been used to kill Mr Sinclair at a distance of less than four feet. He had died in the kitchen of the house. The lounge had evidence of some disturbance, but otherwise the house had not been subject to a burglar's search. It was assumed that the defendants had been disturbed by Mr Sinclair and one of them had shot him. A wrist watch belonging to Mr Sinclair was missing and had not been found. Darren's friends had both testified that the gun belonged to Darren and all three protested their innocence. They did not have a satisfactory alibi for where they were on the night of the murder, but Big Ben knew where they had been for some part of the night, and he was not going give them an alibi.

They protested their innocence right up to and after they had been found guilty by the twelve good and true men and women. Darren's two friends were sent down for twenty years, Darren for twenty-five

There was one possible flaw in her plan which had added to her worries intensely, and that was that if the police were to have investigated more thoroughly they might, only might, have found out about the previous animosity between Bill and Agnes. But Bill had never told his wife about, 'that one' in the office whom he had come to despise. Bill was a paragon of virtue to his wife, and as far as she knew, he was a model manager at work, the enmity connection between Bill and Agnes was never discovered. The newspapers painted Darren as thoroughly evil, and Bill as a diligent manager and honest, family man.

Two months into his sentence, Darren was still claiming innocence and there was talk of an appeal. Agnes felt that she had to do something about that in case someone started to believe him. Such a possibility had not been part of her original plan. She had heard of prisoners being roughed up while in prison, sometimes for 'Grassing', and sometimes for 'Crossing' a man like Big Ben.

She knew that Darren had 'Crossed' Big Ben, so she set out to exploit this information by making regular walks through Ben's domain. As she hoped it was not long before she was accosted by him and his henchmen.

He stood in front of her with a menacing posture and said, "You are the Aunt of that murderer Darren aren't you?"

Faltering, as she had practiced lots of times, she stammered, "Yes but I wanted nothing to do with him."

He grabbed her arm and gave it a twist, "We think your nephew and his two mates helped themselves to a large piece of our action, d'you knows anything about it?"

Agnes did not speak but was frightened more than she had expected to be. Her arm felt as if it was broken but he twisted it more. She had not wished for a broken arm.

"Come on y' bitch, what d'you know about it? Did that nephew of yours have anything to do with it?"

Sheepishly she said, "If it's that night you came to my house, I don't know anything."

He wrenched her arm almost out of its socket saying, "We know it must have been him, he had a gun, so tell us, or you lose your arm!"

Again, this time in great pain, she screamed, "I don't know anything, but that night when you came to my house they had been up to something and they had a red sports bag. I didn't see what was in the bag. I only know that I heard one of them say, 'He will kill us if he finds out.' I suppose it was you they were talking about but they took the bag away, they said they would wait for it to cool."

Ben had fire in his eyes when he said, "A red bag! That will be our stuff, where did they take it?"

She again feigned ignorance and he let her arm free, at the same time throwing her to the ground. He was obviously in a blistering temper.

As she was getting up with her sore arm and bruised knees he said, "We'll show that clever sod that if he crosses Big Ben he pays for it, and he'll pay dearly."

Agnes denied any further knowledge of the bag or its contents and clutching her aching arm, went home hoping that the pain would be worth it.

A month later she read in the newspaper, 'Darren the drinking killer has met with a fatal accident in prison. The authorities are investigating the possibility of foul play. Suspicion has been aroused because his two accomplices to the murder have been involved in accidents within the last week.'

Agnes slept soundly, not having the slightest nightmare, but pleasurable, recurring visions of Bill's face on seeing her at his back door, dressed in Darren's overalls; a skull cap over her hair; wearing boots, and, of course, Marigold gloves.

She recalled the look of surprise and then fear on his face when she invited herself into the kitchen with the gun pointing at him, and said, "Hello Mr Sinclair, I have come to settle some debts". He was frightened out of his wits. He did not say the usual film line of, "You would not dare to use that." No, he could not say that. He could not say anything, he was so frightened. He knew the enmity that she had towards him and many was the bitter score to settle. She asked him, "Do you remember the time you hauled me up before the boss for not reporting my absence when my mother died? I do. You were smirking in his office when I was squirming."

She was shaking with nerves and struggling to keep her composure, wondering if she would have the strength to pull the trigger. She put two hands on the gun to give her two-finger purchase, but never did it cross her mind that she would not kill him. He, in turn, had gone as white, as a sheet but he never moved, seemingly rooted to the floor or paralysed.

"That was only one of dozens times that you tormented me. You were proud of yourself, showing the boss that you had disciplining qualities. You tried hard to get my scalp on your belt. That would have been an accolade for you." She continued, "I am going to savour these moments forever."

Her nerves were saying: get on with it; she had to get it done and be back in case the boys returned. She held the gun up about two meters from his face and squeezed the trigger.

It was not as difficult as she had thought. In fact she remembered with pleasure the way he fell flat on his face, as she had many times hoped he metaphorically would. There seemed to be very little blood

Then there was the end game to play. Get out of the house and wait to see if anyone had heard the shot. Nobody seemed to have. All was silent. Wrap the gun up try to preserve fingerprints. Get back down the track to the station and perhaps wait to see that it was clear before she emerged.

She had left a black bin bag about twenty meters from the station. In it she had left a light coat and shoes. She changed her footwear and put the boots in the bag. With the coat covering the overalls she made her way back home.

At home she removed the coat and the overalls before entering the rear door, the boots were placed in the outhouse, where they had been for some weeks. The overalls and skull cap and thick socks were placed in the bin bag and then in the bin with the Marigolds. The bin was due to be collected the next morning and she had no reason to think that it would not be emptied on time this week.

She entered the house barefoot placing her shoes in the washbasin to be washed; she stripped, placed the coat and other apparel in the washer and then showered. Then last of all she had returned the gun to the loft.

In due course Agnes received her money from the police. Darren had not been brought to account for stealing from her The Inspector had advised her against wishing to press charges.

Four months later she was scanning the 'Horse and Hound' and noticed, 'Melton Mowbray. Assistant to a Vet required to feed animals and to clean the kennels and cattery. Rented Mews accommodation would be available.' She thought, that is just what I want to get me away from here and into oblivion.

She applied for the job and secured the post. She lost some money selling her house on a quick sale, which she sold with the instructions to the estate agent that he must not to put any signs outside of her property.

Considering £122,000 to be reasonable, she moved away as if doing a moonlight flit. No forwarding address was given and, as they say, she lived happily ever after, with her dog; her two pensions; a job she liked with animals, and close to a two-hundred grand nest egg, but she still had one small problem. How does, or did, Big Ben wash his dirty drugs money? She needed now to wash £30,000 plus, of it.

* * *

MORE SIMILARLY SILLY SIMILES FOR BIGGER CHILDREN

I'm as happy as a firefly with evanescent light,
And as happy as a barn owl who, we know is erudite.
I'm as unhappy like a fruit-bat cos' it's really rather blind,
I'm as happy as the little mice that frighten womankind.

I'm as lonely as a mocking bird, they say he's quite sardonic,
But I'm happy as a cuckoo, whose call is quite laconic.
I'm as tough as a hippo with his pachydermous skin,
I'm unhappy like a stick insect that's very, very thin.

I'm as delighted as a Zebra with his much striated coat,
I'm a happy little deer, I get a new coat when I molt.
As a most important house-cat I'm fastidious with my coat,
But mine is made of ermine and I'm a little stoat.

I'm as happy as a codfish with his silver squamous skin.
I'm as busy as a Pelican, who garners fishes in his chin.
I'm as happy as a whale is, with its physique mesomorphous
And a rhinoceros is like him, you know he's quite enormous.

I'm as sad as any giraffe is, with a touch of tonsillitis,
Even worse would be nightingale if she had laryngitis.
I suppose that's better than having itchy dermatitis,
But no-one wants a liver with a bit of hepatitis.

I'm as happy as a woodworm with diet xylophagous
Woodpeckers pick them out with a beak that's xylotomous
I'm happy like a chameleon with a skin that's polychromous
And if you understand these words you're not an ignoramus

The PC and Elf-n-safety brigade, insist that all classes and courses should be made aware of the safety policy. In spite of the previous Safety Villanelle it was incumbent upon the teacher to ensure that students were mindful of the hazards that were around us.

How then could a writer be in need of a safety policy?

A stab wound with a pencil? Cut a finger on a pencil sharpener? Doze off and fall off his or her perch? Get writer's cramp, or be hit with a writer's block? Should we worry that anyone writing about the Mafia could be 'Rubbed' out?

Perhaps the potential injury may not be physical but mental? I know that when I received my 200th refusal from a publisher I was mortified. A bit late for safety you might think when one is necrotic. But, like the best horror stories, I revived, and without needing mouth-to-mouth resuscitation. This mouth-to-mouth stuff led me to think that I might write a love story. So I felt that I had to research, at least, the mouth-to-mouth bit. This seemed quite pleasurable at first. I did not need to travel as most of the action occurred right under my nose.

While doing this research I later found that I was laying myself open to pneumonia, pneumonic plague, herpes, thrush, glandular fever or many other transmittable contagions, even AIDS. Realising the inherent safety hazards of this love stuff, I soon dismissed all ideas of a block-buster love story.

Then there was the time when I was midshipman to Nelson on his ship 'The Victory', (only in the story of course) Research for that was strenuous. Besides being stricken with 'Sea Fever' one could receive a nasty crack on the cranium when the boom came over. The safety manual aboard ship is quite comprehensive. Nelson, of course, being an Admiral, ignored it, and you remember how he fared. He should have read the manual before he lost his eye and then he carelessly lost an arm, before he walked into a bullet.

Research was no less arduous when I wrote, what should have been a best seller, about the fishing fleet. Getting one's feet caught in the nets; slipping on dead fish; keeping up the Mae West, and looking as top heavy as Dolly Parton was a must. Slitting fish open with cold wet fingers was disgusting; it needed lots of guts and I didn't have enough.

I must tell you about the oil rigs. What with spanners dropping from the sky; 80 mile-an-hour gales; Mae West around your chest, gas leaks and fire drills, it was difficult to find time to write. I am sure that those heavy Toe-Tector boots with their steel toe-caps would have taken me, Mae West and Dolly Parton straight to the bottom if I had been unfortunate enough to be swept off the rig. That is why I haven't written a block-buster about the Oilmen.

When I was a big Union Boss (in a car factory yarn) the research required me always to be outside the yellow lines as I moved about the factory floor. Welding could result in burns. Fumes causing ozena were prevalent, and electrocution was not far away from a 'bright spark' like me if I had not been careful. Constantly the world had to be viewed through smoked glasses or a smoked visor. No story with a rose-tinted ending there.

Research into the mining industry might have given me a good, Klondike yarn. But I found myself to be in a right hole, exposing my lungs to all manner of diseases. I found that continual inhalation of the dust could bring on silicosis which in turn causes a chronic shortness of breath. I have heard that people die of shortness of breath. I was a minor among miners. I had expected that they could throw some light on the subject but they had such small lamps and all those miners gave me black looks. There was no golden opportunity for a block-buster there.

The scariest bit of research was into polar exploration, when I was with Scott of the Antarctic. It seemed to be a suitable theme. But that idea was doomed to failure from the start. Every time I needed to go outside I thought of that unfortunate man Evans, who went outside and he died. I got cold feet when I considered the consequence of getting frost bite. The special diet needed to keep hypothermia at bay included large amounts of cod liver oil. This in turn can induce hypervitaminosis 'A', from consuming too much Vitamin A. The risks were never ending. Just as the miners had shunned me, this lot gave me the cold shoulder.

All my researches have led me to conclude that the safest place for a writer would be in bed. That is assuming one can avoid the bed sores and a tendency to get a little callous.

There's a thought. "A Life In Pyjamas' I'll try that.

ODE TO A TEACHER

I've attended every lesson and I've done it faithfully,
Ideas I've had to jettison but continued dolefully.
I revised and I polished I tried every poet's style,
You can tell how hard I practised by the thickness of my file.

Writing poetry is quite easy if it does not have to rhyme,
I can knock off twenty stanzas in a very little '*moment.*'
It does not take much effort; you don't need a lot of brain,
I can do it over and over, and over, and over '*and over.*'

We learnt about the Sonnet with its pentameter feet,
It took a lot of effort but I think mine rather neat,
In fact it was quite stressful cos I stressed on the wrong foot,
When teacher pointed out this fault I had to substitute.

The Villanelle with its lines repeating,
Has thirty feet that I cannot make scan.
To repeat a line, that's sort of cheating.

Hours and hours with my brain overheating.
If I were the laureate I would ban.
The Villanelle with its lines repeating.

I would not succeed with abrogating.
Because it's par for an Oxonian.
To repeat a line, that's sort of cheating.

Free verse, however, is something I wot not.
The lines are all of differing length.
No rhymes. in sight,
Confused? Me?
Yes.

Lisa, this is not meant to make you sad,
Nor even to make you in anyway mad.
Please do not think you wasted time,
But the poetry I like just has to rhyme.

Lightning Source UK Ltd.
Milton Keynes UK
UKHW02f1104010818
326605UK00005B/212/P